called of **GOD**

Kenneth Hagin Jr.

First Printing 2007

ISBN–13: 978-0-89276-747-2
ISBN–10: 0-89276-747-2

In the U.S. write:
Kenneth Hagin Ministries
P.O. Box 50126
Tulsa, OK 74150-0126
1-888-28-FAITH
www.rhema.org

In Canada write:
Kenneth Hagin Ministries
P.O. Box 335, Station D
Etobicoke (Toronto), Ontario
Canada, M9A 4X3
www.rhemacanada.org

contents

preface

According to the Bible, every believer has been given a ministry of reconciliation (2 Cor. 5:18). That means that God has called each of us in the Body of Christ to fulfill a specific purpose on this earth.

However, there are also those whom God calls to make the ministry their life's purpose. Of course, this includes what we call the fivefold or pulpit ministry (Eph. 4:11). But it also can include those in supportive ministries or the ministry of helps, which is a scriptural, valid ministry (1 Cor. 12:28).

I have been actively involved in ministry and with ministers all of my life. In fact, I was born one Sunday and in church the next Sunday!

As president of RHEMA Bible Training Center, I have desired for many years to help those who are called to the ministry of the Lord Jesus Christ fulfill their highest destiny. I have learned much from ministers who have gone before. Thank God for older, seasoned ministers of the Gospel who can help others make a successful entrance and passage into purposeful ministry for our Lord Jesus Christ. I am especially grateful to my father, Rev. Kenneth E. Hagin, and my father-in-law, Rev. V.E. Tipton, for the example they set before me and the lessons they taught me.

In this book I've endeavored to share scriptural principles, learned through many years of ministerial experience, that can help you succeed in the ministry God has called you to fulfill.

Whether you are called to preach or to help in some area, there is much to glean from these biblical principles to help you along the road to success in the ministry!

Personally, I believe one of the reasons for the growth of the Pentecostal-Charismatic move in Christianity is that the truth of the baptism in the Holy Spirit helps every Christian quickly understand he is potentially capable of ministry. While the distinction between pulpit ministry and the laity has blinded much of the Body of Jesus Christ and kept them from getting involved in ministry, Charismatics have viewed themselves as potential ministers in any situation.

The word *ministry* means "service." Since the time of Constantine, when the difference between laity and clergy was emphasized, Christians have separated the work of ministry from the Body of Jesus Christ. In this book, there is a purposeful overlap between the ministry gifts and supportive ministry.

In the pages that follow, when I discuss ministry, I am talking about the more general term, rather than the popular term applied to pulpit preachers and teachers. Since the word *ministry* is the same as "service"—and to minister means to serve—my discussion will focus on the wider understanding of ministry. So whether you're sensing a call to pulpit ministry or more hands-on supportive ministry, this book will help you understand the nature of your call to ministry.

Kenneth Hagin Jr.

the call of **GOD** in this hour

part one

heeding
the call

my personal motto has always been, "I cannot be defeated, and I will not quit!" To succeed in the ministry, you have to take the word *quit* out of your vocabulary. Personally, the word *quit* doesn't exist in my life or ministry. Let me give you an example in the natural realm to show you what I mean.

My son, Craig, and I used to race motorcycles. One of the races was so difficult that only 100 out of 300 entrants finished the race.

I was sorely tempted to quit in the middle of that race. At one point, I tried to pull my motorcycle out of the mud for what seemed like the millionth time. But I was so tired, all I could do was drag it a short distance. Then I collapsed on the ground to rest for a while before I lugged it a little farther. I finally got it on dry ground where I could start it again. But by then I was so tired, I just flopped on the ground to rest.

As I lay there resting, the thought went through my mind, *Why don't you just quit? You can just lie here, and eventually someone will come by to pick you up and take you back to the starting point.*

But I declared out loud, "No! I'm not going to quit!" And I made myself get up. I was tired, thirsty, and covered with mud, but I started my motorcycle and got back in the race.

Not far up the trail, I came to another rough stretch called "Lester's Tester." It was a narrow trail that was nothing but one switchback after another through a forest, making it easy for me to lose my balance or hit a tree. I don't know how many times I fell down and had to get back on the motorcycle and start again. But I still refused to quit.

All of a sudden I came to a slick place on the trail. My back tires slipped off the trail, and I slid down a 10-foot embankment into the river! By that time, I was so exhausted, I couldn't even hold the motorcycle upright as I slid down the hill. I just plunged right into the water.

Now I was not only muddy, tired, and thirsty—I was *wet*! I lay down on the side of that riverbank and inwardly groaned, "Now I have to pull this bike back up the hill! Oh, Lord, help!"

My mind said, "Would you please just quit! This is ridiculous!"

But I said, "No, I *won't* quit! I'm going to finish this race. I'm *not* going to be a quitter!"

Somehow I got that motorcycle up that embankment and went on to finish that race. The officials gave everyone who finished a button that I still have because it reminds me never to quit. Even though I didn't win that race, in my own mind I was a winner, because I overcame the temptation to quit and finished what I started, despite all obstacles.

It's not that the race was so important. I refused to quit because I represent the Lord, He has a job for me to do, and I don't want "quit" associated with Him or myself.

You have to do that in the ministry too. Don't quit on God. He won't quit on you! If you're called, you're called—no matter how bad circumstances look or how tired you get. As you're faithful to your call, God will honor your obedience and help you finish your appointed course.

You may ask, "How do I know I'm called to the ministry?" God does not call every Christian to the fivefold ministry positions listed in Ephesians 4:11. But he does call some, because those offices are needed in the Body of Christ (see Eph. 4:12.) The Lord also calls some Christians into other types of ministry as listed in First Corinthians 12:28. The ministry of helps is included here, and it is a valid ministry!

My dad used to say that if you're called to preach, you know it. You don't go into the ministry just because you want to. He knew as a little kid that he was called. When adults would ask him and his brothers what they wanted to be when they grew up, he'd say, "I a peacher." He meant, "I'm a preacher."

Dad said he used to go out to his grandpa's garden and preach to the cabbage heads. (He used to joke sometimes that, at times, it seemed like he was still preaching to cabbage heads!) In the winter, when it was cold and there was no garden, he'd climb up into the barn loft and preach to the bales of hay. He'd say, "If you've got the preach in you, it's going to come out!"

For my dad, God's calling was an inward knowing. Dad said he knew on the inside that the Lord's call to the ministry was on his life. He didn't know everything involved with it. He just knew it was there.

Be sure you are in the ministry because *God* called you, not because your parents or your pastor told you that you'd make a good preacher. When Satan tries to buffet you with pressures and problems, it will be an anchor for you to know beyond a shadow of a doubt that God is the One Who called you.

Sometimes I think about the night God called me. It was at a New Year's Eve prayer service, and I was 11 years old. At 20 minutes before midnight, the pastor called us all forward to pray around the altar. As I was praying at the altar, I heard God speak to me in my heart as distinctly as I've ever heard anyone's voice. The Lord told me that He was calling me to the ministry.

I didn't want to hear that. I had already decided I was going to live for God—but I *didn't* want to be a minister! So mentally I put God's call on a shelf in the back of my mind, and for several years I tried to ignore it. I reasoned that as long as I didn't get *too* close to God, He wouldn't bother me about His call.

But when I was 17 years old, the Lord confirmed His call on my life. I was attending a youth camp in the California mountains. One evening we watched a missionary film called *Beyond the Bells*. It was about a missionary who diligently ministered to a tribe of American Indians for seven years without any apparent results before he finally began reaping a harvest of souls.

The Lord used that missionary film to speak to my heart. After the film was over, all the other teenagers in the room left to go do other things. I went into a side room, knelt beside a bunk bed, buried my face in the mattress, and began to pray.

That night I stopped running away from the call of God. When I got up off my knees, I knew beyond a shadow of a doubt that I would obey God's call to the ministry. And I made that decision on my own, without any help or pressure from my parents.

In fact, my dad wouldn't even talk to me about my call to the ministry until later, after I had publicly acknowledged it. When he and I finally did discuss God's call on my life, Dad explained why he'd kept silent about the matter for so long.

Dad told me, "I couldn't talk to you about going into the ministry until you had determined God's call on your life for yourself. Your decision to answer the call had to be between you and God. That way, when the pressure comes and the going gets rough, you won't be tempted to give up and think, *It must have been Dad instead of God who convinced me I should go into the ministry.*"

Dad was wise. I often relive my personal experience with God the night I accepted His call. That experience helps me hold steady and stay committed to my call when the pressure is on.

Perhaps at some point in *your* life, God made His call clear to you. You realize life is not about you. You desire to give yourself to His greater purposes for your life. That call is unmistakable, and now you may be asking yourself, "What do I do with this call?"

First, you must realize that *training for ministry is not an option.* It will be difficult for you to fully accomplish what

God wants you to do without preparation. It is very unlikely that God will place a person in a responsible position of ministry if he or she is not prepared or equipped for it. First Timothy 3:6 indicates that a novice should not be considered for a position in full-time ministry. A novice means one who is unskilled, untrained, or *unprepared.*

To prepare for ministry, you would do well to attend a good Bible school. And among Bible schools, of course, I can personally recommend RHEMA Bible Training Center. Attending RHEMA is an excellent way for you to prepare yourself spiritually and determine what God has called you to do. RHEMA can help equip you to fulfill God's call on your life.

Perhaps you have a desire to do more for God but are not sure that He has called you to a pulpit ministry, so you're wondering what to do. Whenever someone told my father they were facing this dilemma, and they asked him what they should do, he would tell them to get a solid foundation in the Word of God.

RHEMA Bible Training Center was founded to give people a solid grounding in God's Word and in the working of the Holy Spirit. Dad would tell people who weren't sure they were called to ministry to come to RHEMA and get trained in the Word and in the Spirit. He'd say the training would bless them, even if God hadn't called them to preach or teach. The training RHEMA provides would make them much better laborers when they returned to their local churches. As Dad often used to say, "Preparation time is never wasted time."

you are
chosen of GOD

If you have ever sensed the call of God to the ministry of the Lord Jesus Christ, consider yourself greatly privileged. You are God's choice to share His Word on this earth and help equip the Body of Christ in these last days.

The work of the ministry is manifested in many different ways. For example, some people are called to missions work, some to pastor, some to lead Bible studies, and others to work in the helps or supportive ministry. But regardless of what capacity you're called to fulfill, Jesus Christ gives you the same invitation He gives to every person He calls to His service: "*. . . FOLLOW Me, and I WILL MAKE YOU BECOME FISHERS OF MEN*" (Mark 1:17).

Although God personalizes the call to the ministry to fit each person's unique personality, the call is always essentially the same. In other words, to be called of God is to be given the task of seeking out those who are unsaved or hurting. Then with the net of God's love, a true minister pulls people from the sea of sin and defeat into the boat of salvation and abundant life.

Since the beginning of time, God has always chosen people to carry out His will on this earth. Throughout the centuries ever since Adam sinned, God has handpicked people to proclaim His plan of redemption. He's chosen men and women to lead others into the path of righteousness.

For instance, Noah was God's choice for his generation. The Bible calls Noah a "preacher of righteousness" (2 Peter 2:5). As Noah prepared the ark, he must have warned the people to repent, knowing God would soon bring the Flood upon the earth in judgment of sin.

Moses: **GOD**'s choice to deliver Israel

The Bible tells us about men and women whom God chose to accomplish His purpose before they were ever born (Jer. 1:5). Moses was one of those people. He was God's choice to deliver the Israelites from Egyptian bondage and lead them into the Promised Land.

So how does Moses' life relate to you? Moses was God's choice for his generation, but *you* are one of God's chosen for this generation!

Moses was born at a time when Pharaoh had decreed that every Hebrew male child was to be killed (Exod. 1:22). But despite man's decree, the baby Moses was *not* destroyed, because he was God's choice—God's instrument of deliverance—to speak to his generation!

In the midst of seeming impossibilities, God not only spared Moses from destruction, but He also made a way for Moses' own mother to take care of him and raise him in the knowledge of God (Exod. 2:1–9)! Moses went on to become well-educated in all the ways of the Egyptians (Exod. 2:10). Throughout Moses' youth, God's hand was upon him to train him for God's future purposes.

Moses grew up in Pharaoh's own house. When Moses walked down the city streets as a young man, he wore royal clothing, and people everywhere honored him as a person of prominence. But the day came when God told him, "Moses, I've chosen you to deliver My people. You have to make a choice. Who are you going to serve—Me or the pleasures of this world?" The Bible says Moses had to choose between "suffering affliction with the people of God" or enjoying "the treasures of Egypt" (Heb. 11:25–26).

Moses came to a crossroads in his life one day when he saw an Egyptian beating a slave—one of his Israelite brothers. Moses killed the Egyptian (Exod. 2:11–12). That act forced Moses to run from Pharaoh's wrath, and he ended up far away in the desert land of Midian.

So there was God's choice—the highly trained and well-educated Moses—stuck on the backside of the wilderness, seemingly far removed from what he was called to do! Things must have looked quite hopeless for Moses, the supposed deliverer of Israel.

Forty long years passed. In the meantime, Moses married a Midianite woman and worked for his father-in-law tending sheep. Then one day as Moses was herding sheep on Mount Horeb, God communicated with him, His chosen deliverer.

EXODUS 3:2,7–8,10
2 And the Angel of the Lord appeared to him [Moses] in a flame of fire from the midst of a bush. So he looked, and behold, the bush was burning with fire, but the bush was not consumed. . . .

7 And the Lord said: "I have surely seen the oppression of My people who are in Egypt, and have heard their cry because of their taskmasters, for I know their sorrows.

 8 "So I have come down to deliver them out of the hand of the Egyptians, and to bring them up from that land to a good and large land, to a land flowing with milk and honey, to the place of the Canaanites and the Hittites and the Amorites and the Perizzites and the Hivites and the Jebusites. . . .

10 "Come now, therefore, and I WILL SEND YOU TO PHA-RAOH THAT YOU MAY BRING MY PEOPLE, THE CHILDREN OF ISRAEL, OUT OF EGYPT."

You see, even during those 40 long years, God knew just where to find Moses. The backside of the desert wasn't too far away for God! And when the time was right, God communicated to Moses what He wanted him to do. He basically told Moses, "All right, son. You've been out in the wilderness long enough. It's time to answer your call!"

God knows where you are too! And no matter where you are, God can communicate with you. God has chosen you, and no matter how far you might try to run away from the call of God or how impossible fulfilling that call may seem to be, the Lord always knows just where to find you.

If you'll seek God, He will communicate with you so you'll know step by step what He wants you to do in the ministry. But *you* will have to choose whether to obey His call.

For example, when God told Moses what He wanted him to do, at first Moses reacted in the natural. It seemed impossible for him to accomplish God's plan: *"But Moses said to God, 'Who am I that I should go to Pharaoh, and that I should bring the children of Israel out of Egypt?'"* (Exod. 3:11).

But the Lord had a good answer for Moses' argument: "*. . . I WILL CERTAINLY BE WITH YOU. . . . Thus you shall say to the children of Israel, 'I AM has sent me to you'*" (Exod. 3:12,14).

Later Moses argued with the Lord again about his commission to deliver the Israelites from Egypt, saying, "*'But suppose they will not believe me or listen to my voice; suppose they say, "The Lord has not appeared to you"'*" (Exod. 4:1).

Notice how God answered Moses this time: "*So the Lord said to him, 'What is that in your hand?' He said, 'A ROD'*" (Exod. 4:2).

The Lord told Moses to throw the rod on the ground. When Moses obeyed, it turned into a serpent. Then the Lord told Moses to pick up the serpent by the tail. Moses did, and the serpent once more became a rod in his hand (Exod. 4:3–4).

By this supernatural demonstration, the Lord showed Moses that *He* would perform the impossible through Moses. The great *I AM* would perform miracles to display His glory and power through the simple rod in Moses' hand (Exod. 3:14).

So Moses obeyed the Lord and returned to Egypt with his family. And the Bible says that as he started on his journey, he took the rod of God in his hand.

EXODUS 4:20–21
20 Then Moses took his wife and his sons and set them on a donkey, and he returned to the land of Egypt. AND MOSES TOOK THE ROD OF GOD IN HIS HAND.
21 And the Lord said to Moses, "When you go back to Egypt, see that you do all those wonders before Pharaoh WHICH I HAVE PUT IN YOUR HAND. . . .

In other words, Moses returned to Egypt in the power and authority of God.

your rod in ministry

It was Moses' rod that represented God's anointing and power. Moses used that rod many times, and God performed signs and wonders as He supernaturally led the Israelites out of Egypt and through the wilderness.

What does the rod of God in Moses' hand have to do with you and me? We don't have a physical rod, but we do possess what that rod stood for—the authority of God's anointed Word.

As one chosen to help proclaim the Gospel, you hold the rod of God—His Word—in your hand. God's Word contains His infinite power. In fact, the Bible says God's Word *is* His power unto salvation to those who believe (Rom. 1:16).

You can tap into the power in God's Word by sowing the seed of the incorruptible Word into people's hearts. The Word will produce miracles in people's lives as they receive it in faith.

The rod of God's Word also works when you plant it in your own heart. The Word enables you to fulfill God's call on your life in victory. The Word causes the anointing of God's Spirit to increase in your life and ministry.

The rod of God's anointed Word gives you authority over the enemy's attacks and obstacles. As Moses hit the rock in the wilderness, causing the water to pour forth (Exod. 17:5–6), so you can hit the rock of circumstances with the rod of God's Word. And as you act in faith on the truth of God's Word, the fountain of God's victory and blessings will flow.

When you come up against the Red Sea on one side and Pharaoh's army on the other—*your* impenetrable barriers and difficult problems—you can use God's Word, and the hindrances will move out of your way so you can cross to the other side to victory.

You are chosen of God to herald the message of salvation through Jesus Christ so that His Name may be glorified in the earth. God's power has been made available to you to fulfill your call through the rod of God—the eternal, unchanging Word of the living God.

So what are you going to do with the rod of God? You have a responsibility to do the same thing God told Moses to do: "Take the rod and go back to Egypt" (Exod. 4:17,19)!

Egypt is a type of the world. It represents those who are living in bondage to Satan, sin, sickness, and disease. You are one of God's chosen ministers, and He is telling *you* to return to Egypt—to the lost and hurting people of this world—and set them free with the truth of the Gospel.

When you accepted the call of God to the ministry, you took up the rod of God's Word in your hand, just as Moses took up that physical rod. And as you answer the call of God on your life, God will train you so you'll know what to do with the rod of His Word He's given you.

skillfully using the rod of **GOD**'s word

As you endeavor to answer God's call on your life, you'll sometimes encounter obstacles in your path. Obstacles can make fulfilling your call seem like a distant, unreachable goal. At times like that, it's easy to lose track of the divine purpose you're pursuing.

You might wonder: "Why are these tests and trials coming against me? I thought I was in God's perfect will by answering His call. I'd rather just lead a nice, quiet, normal life. Answering the call to the ministry is too hard!"

If you find yourself thinking those kinds of thoughts, that's the time to give yourself a pep talk. Tell yourself:

"I refuse to think that way, because I'm chosen of God! He has given me the rod of His Word, and I've accepted His call to the ministry. I'm going to fulfill His purpose for my life!"

Realize that every minister, no matter how successful, has encountered problems and difficulties along the way. And you're mistaken if you think *you're* going to be the only exception!

For instance, look at Paul's life. Paul was God's choice to carry the Gospel to the Gentiles.

Paul was well-equipped academically to succeed in life. He'd studied at the feet of Gamaliel who, according to Jewish historians, was one of the greatest rabbis who ever lived.

After his conversion, Paul became a great man of faith. He wrote more about faith than anyone else in the Bible. But did Paul go through life never encountering any tests or trials? That's not what I read in the Bible!

2 CORINTHIANS 11:24–28

24 From the Jews five times I received forty stripes minus one.
25 Three times I was beaten with rods; once I was stoned; three times I was shipwrecked; a night and a day I have been in the deep;
26 in journeys often, in perils of waters, in perils of robbers, in perils of my own countrymen, in perils of the Gentiles, in perils in the city, in perils in the wilderness, in perils in the sea, in perils among false brethren;
27 in weariness and toil, in sleeplessness often, in hunger and thirst, in fastings often, in cold and nakedness—
28 besides the other things, what comes upon me daily: my deep concern for all the churches.

That doesn't sound much like flowery beds of ease, does it? No, as Paul obeyed God's call, he experienced hardships that he'd never encountered before. But he also experienced times of great fulfillment and joy.

The same will be true in your life. You *will* face opposition from the enemy as he tries to keep you from fulfilling your call to the ministry. But as you obey God, great joy and rewards also await you—not only in this life, but also in the life to come.

Yes, you are chosen of God, and you hold the powerful rod of God's Word in your hand. But the Bible also says the devil roams about, seeking whom he may devour (1 Peter 5:8). Satan wants to keep you from using the rod of God to set people free. He'll try to stop you before you ever get started.

That's why you need to give the Word first place in your life. The rod of God's Word will keep you strong in faith and help you overcome the enemy's opposition.

There's an old saying, "To be forewarned is to be forearmed." Hide God's Word in your heart so you can be forearmed against the devil's strategies in your life and ministry!

The devil will try to hinder you whenever he can. That's what he did when Moses returned to Egypt and God began working miracles through Moses with the rod of God. Every time God wrought a miracle through Moses, Satan tried to match it.

For instance, when Moses threw his rod on the ground before Pharaoh and it turned into a serpent, Pharaoh called for his magicians. When the magicians threw their rods on the ground, their rods also became serpents (Exod. 7:10–12).

But what happened *then* shows the difference between God's power and Satan's. Moses' serpent swallowed up all the magicians' serpents! Then once again, it became a rod in Moses' hand. You see, the devil has some power, but he's always the loser when he tries to come against the power of God. God's power is far greater than the power of the devil!

So don't be afraid of the devil! When God calls and equips you, you can be confident that the gates of hell cannot withstand you as you obey God.

Just be aware of how the enemy works. As you answer God's call to the ministry, you'll find out that he'll try to match you step for step. Every time you gain new ground for the Lord, Satan will try to match it with a strategy to make you lose ground.

That's why you must always keep in mind that you're chosen of God and that you're more than a conqueror in Christ! The Lord has chosen you to do a work, and as you hold fast to the rod of God's Word, God will help you overcome every strategy of the enemy.

Keep trusting in the Lord with all your heart. Exercise the authority that's in the rod of God's Word. Then one day, you'll expect to see the devil trying to match you stride for stride the way he used to, but he won't be there. He'll be far behind you in the dust of God's power, unable to catch up with you or defeat you! As you continue to make God's Word your strength, you'll outstride the devil every time!

Satan's power is no match for God's power! Greater is He Who is in you than he that is in the world (1 John 4:4).

you are a victor in Christ!

God's power always proved greater than the devil's attacks in Paul's life too. In the face of the many tests and trials Paul encountered as he followed God, Paul still proclaimed, ". . . *thanks be to God who ALWAYS LEADS US IN TRIUMPH IN CHRIST. . .*" (2 Cor. 2:14).

How could Paul say that when he had to deal with so many problems? Because Paul was really declaring, "I am chosen of God. I possess the rod of God—the authority of

God's holy Word. I've been given a job to do, and in Christ, I am a victor over all obstacles. I *will* do what God has called me to do!"

When Paul faced imprisonment, shipwrecks, and every opposition, the devil probably told him, "You don't *look* like a victor!" But Paul stood strong on God's Word, believing that God would cause him to triumph in *every* situation.

When you face hardship and difficulties in the ministry, the devil will try to make you admit defeat. What will you do if he whispers to your mind, "You don't look like a victor!"

Do the same thing Paul did. Stand steadfast on God's Word and say, "Thanks be to God, I'm God's chosen vessel. I've accepted the call and the challenge of God to the ministry. And no matter what my natural circumstances look like, God always causes me to triumph. I *am* a victor!"

GOD never relinquishes the call; neither should you!

Despite all opposition, hold fast in faith to the fulfillment of God's call on your life. *Esteem* your call to the ministry. The ministry is a sacred and holy calling and should never be taken lightly.

You must realize that whatever God has called you to do in the ministry, He will never relinquish that call. The Bible says the gifts and calling of God are *without repentance* (Rom. 11:29 *KJV*). He will not revoke them. That divine call is on your life whether you decide to obey it or not.

Look at the biblical example of King Saul. Saul chose *not* to obey God, and his rebellion cost him the anointing of God on his life. But Saul didn't start out being disobedient to his call.

At first Saul was a humble man who was "little in his own eyes" (1 Sam. 15:17). He was so humble and timid, he even hid when it was time for the prophet Samuel to anoint him as king (1 Sam. 10:21–22).

When Samuel anointed Saul with oil, the anointing and power of God came upon Saul to stand in the office of king. However, later when the Lord instructed Saul to take no spoils or prisoners in the battle with the Amalekites, Saul disobeyed and did exactly the opposite (1 Sam. 15:3,9).

Saul's disobedience caused the rod of God—God's anointing and power—to depart from him (1 Sam. 15:26). *God* didn't do that to Saul. Saul brought judgment upon *himself* through his own sin.

But even though the *anointing* of God to be king had left Saul, the call of God was still on his life (Rom. 11:29). That *call* of God was stirred up in him later when he went to the school of the prophets in Ramah in search of David. The Spirit of God came upon Saul, and he prophesied for a day and a night (1 Sam. 19:23–24).

I've seen the same kind of thing happen to backslidden ministers in our day. Even though they've gotten out of fellowship with God, sometimes when they come together with other believers where the Spirit of God is moving, that call is stirred up in them. I've seen backslidden preachers get up and operate in the gifts of the Spirit or give an exhortation so skillfully, you'd think they were the most spiritual people in the world!

That happens because God does not withdraw His gifts and calling. God is just waiting for them to repent and get back into fellowship with Him. Unfortunately, many never yield to the call, and they walk away from God, never to return.

Don't be caught in that sad situation yourself. God has ordained His purpose for your life before the foundations of the world (Eph. 1:4; 2:10). He alone knows what is best for you. So make it easy on yourself and yield quickly to His call.

If God has called you, there isn't any way for you to get away from that call. Paul understood that fact. He said, *"For if I preach the gospel, I have nothing to boast of, for necessity is laid upon me; yes, woe is me if I do not preach the gospel!"* (1 Cor. 9:16).

I don't care how far you run or how many doors you lock behind you, God knows where you are and what He has called you to do. The Holy Spirit dwelling within you will gently urge you to answer God's call, because He knows you will never be happy or fulfilled until you do.

what will you do with the rod of **GOD**?

You are God's choice in this generation. The rod of God's Word has been placed within your reach. God has a part for you to play in building His Kingdom in these last days before Jesus returns. After you've allowed God to prepare and train you, you must go to Egypt—to the people who so desperately need Jesus.

You can't stay in a spiritual cocoon, just soaking in God's power and Presence but never doing anything with it. Certainly there is a time to receive instruction from God. But be sensitive to the Holy Spirit so He can tell you when it's time to step into the ministry God has planned for you.

I'm sure Moses would have preferred to stay at the burning bush in the Presence of God's holy power. It would have been wonderful just to rejoice and savor that demonstration of God's glory. But God spoke from the burning bush and instructed Moses, "Take the rod and go back to Egypt!"

When God tells you, "You're ready to go to Egypt," follow Moses' example. Take the rod of God and go forth into the world to do the works of Jesus. Use God's Word to perform miracles by setting people free who are bound and enslaved by Satan, sin, and sickness!

You've been called of God in this hour! God has given you His rod—the authority and power of His Word. Now it's your choice. What are you going to do with God's Word? Are you going to use it only to meet your own needs? Or are you going to take the rod and do the work of the ministry?

What you do with what God has called you to do depends on *you*. It doesn't depend on your parents, your spouse, or your pastor. It doesn't even depend on God because He won't force you to answer His call. He will only gently prompt you on the inside by His Spirit.

You must decide to obey God. Then He will anoint and equip you with all you need to fulfill His call.

As you answer God's sacred and holy call, your commitment to Him will help carry you through both the good times and the hard times. So make this confession from your heart:

I am chosen of God. I have accepted His call, and I will not relinquish it. I will follow God each step of the way and learn all I can.

And I will take the rod, God's anointed Word, and go to those who are bound by Satan and set them free.

That's what I've been called and chosen to do, so I rejoice in my calling!

revival:
the cry of the hour

the call of God on your life gives you a special part in God's glorious plan for revival in this hour. God's primary purpose in these last days is to reach the ends of the earth with the Gospel of Jesus Christ.

So once you've determined to answer God's call to the ministry, get in step with God's heart. You've taken up the rod of God's Word. Now let revival become the cry of your heart!

The truth is, the Spirit of God is already moving mightily in revival on this earth today. In the midst of this growing revival, the Holy Spirit is stirring up and awakening the hearts of supernaturally minded, God-called people.

What are these people awakening to? They are awakening to the call of God to be part of the greatest move of God's Spirit this world has ever known. They are rising up out of every walk of life. From the rich to the poor, from the business executive to the blue-collar worker, God is calling the young and old alike.

Spiritually hungry believers are rising above the fog of tradition and natural thinking by coming into the Presence of God. Their heart's desire is to learn how to walk in the reality of God's supernatural power and glory. They are stirring their hearts up for revival!

recognizing the facts: evil is increasing

If ever we needed our hearts to be stirred up to seek revival, it is now. In these last days before Jesus comes, evil is increasing all around us. Never before have sin, sickness, hatred, strife, wars, famine, and earthquakes occurred on the earth to the degree we see them today.

Evil has been with us since the fall of man. But in our day, sin is openly flaunted to a greater degree than ever before. For instance, sexual sins and perversions have been in this world all the time, but in times past, people usually committed these sins behind closed doors. Today, however, sexual sin is so blatantly splashed on the front pages of newspapers, on prime-time television, and on the Internet that it sickens the hearts of believers.

These may seem like negative statements. But the fact is, they are *true* statements!

Many believers don't like to hear people talk about the reality of sin in the world today. In their desire to confess the promises of God's Word, some believers have gotten into a ditch by trying to ignore the existence of sin in the world and even in their own midst. Sometimes they try to make negative facts go away by refusing to recognize them or by saying, "I won't confess that."

But as my dad, Rev. Kenneth E. Hagin, said to me many times, "Son, you have to look at the negative before you can act on the positive." In other words, you have to take stock of a situation and identify the problem before you can put your faith in God's Word to work in the situation.

Whether or not we confess negative facts, reality is still reality. And until we recognize the facts about the evil in this world, we can't appropriate God's Word to change things.

So what are we doing while evil increases? Some may say, "We're rejoicing in the Lord!" Others say, "We're making our confessions according to the Word." That's good. But the truth is, while we're rejoicing and making our good confessions, people are becoming more and more bound by the devil, and the world is moving toward greater and greater chaos and destruction.

Of course, rejoicing in the Lord and confessing the Word are important to our spiritual walk. But let's make sure we aren't being selfish in our rejoicing and our faith. We should be using our faith to reach others with the Gospel, not just to heap material blessings upon ourselves.

It's not wrong for Christians to believe God to meet their personal needs. But some Christians never attempt to use their faith for *anything or anyone else*!

While many well-meaning Christians are making their faith confessions to get possessions for themselves, every second the clock ticks another person dies somewhere in this world. Did that person know God? Did believers even try to reach him with the Gospel of Jesus Christ? Or were they too busy with their own personal affairs to reach out and tell that one who was on his way to hell about Jesus?

You see, the blessings of God—such as prosperity and divine health—are not the reason the Kingdom of God was established. God's blessings are just fringe benefits. The real reason God established His Kingdom was for the *salvation of mankind.*

Thank God for the blessings He pours out on His children! But let's not lose sight of the true purpose for which we've been called to the ministry. We must fulfill our divine call to bring those who are in bondage to Satan, sin, and sickness into the liberating knowledge of the Gospel of Jesus Christ!

Revival must be the cry of this hour! There is a great harvest of souls that must be won for the Kingdom of God. We must answer the call of God to put aside selfishness and go forth into the world to save those who would otherwise be lost for eternity without God.

operating in the supernatural power of **GOD**

Even though you're called of God to the ministry, that doesn't mean you can make revival happen in your own power. But you *can* rise up and answer your call, equipped with the mighty authority of God's Word and *His* supernatural power. Only then can you overcome the devil's tactics and help reach the world for Jesus in this generation. Yes, the devil has some power, but he's no match for you when you know how to walk in the supernatural power of God!

The Church of the Lord Jesus Christ is rousing itself from spiritual slumber as people hunger for truth and for the demonstration of God's power on the earth. You see, God created man to worship and commune with Him. There's something on the inside of every person that cries out to experience God's supernatural power and Presence. The walls of dead theology and the traditions of man are not strong enough to hold back the hungry soul who is searching for the power of God.

More and more, tradition in the Body of Christ is melting away like snow in the hot sun. Believers whose hearts are hungry for the things of God realize that church traditions are not the answer to the world's desperate needs. They recognize that ministers who just preach nice Bible lessons from the pulpit aren't providing the answers people need.

Spiritually hungry believers look for those who will stand strong and boldly speak the Word of truth with signs and wonders following. They aren't looking for ministers who just dress fancy and give flowery speeches. They aren't interested in listening to ministers who only *talk* about doing the greater works of Jesus, but never do them.

People are eagerly seeking men and women of faith who can teach them by precept and example how to walk in the supernatural power of God! People want true ministers who really know God, like Peter and John whom God used to demonstrate His miraculous power at the Gate called Beautiful.

ACTS 3:1–8
1 Now Peter and John went up together to the temple at the hour of prayer, the ninth hour.
2 And a certain man lame from his mother's womb was carried, whom they laid daily at the gate of the temple which is called Beautiful, to ask alms from those who entered the temple;
3 who, seeing Peter and John about to go into the temple, asked for alms.
4 And fixing his eyes on him, with John, Peter said, "Look at us."
5 So he gave them his attention, expecting to receive something from them.
6 Then Peter said, "Silver and gold I do not have, but WHAT I DO HAVE I GIVE YOU: IN THE NAME OF JESUS CHRIST OF NAZARETH, RISE UP AND WALK."
7 And he took him by the right hand and lifted him up, and immediately his feet and ankle bones received strength.

8 So HE, LEAPING UP, STOOD AND WALKED and entered the temple with them—walking, leaping, and praising God.

After this lame man's miraculous healing, the people rejoiced in the display of God's supernatural power. In fact, after listening to Peter preach the Gospel, five thousand people were saved (Acts 4:4). Revival had begun!

But the Pharisees and the Sadducees, who were the doctors of the Law and the theologians of the day, were upset by what had happened. They told each other, "We can't have this sort of thing going on. It will disturb our religious traditions and undermine our precious authority!"

So these religious leaders called Peter and John in to question them.

ACTS 4:7–8,10,14–18

7 And when they [the religious authorities] had set them [Peter and John] in the midst, they asked, "By what power or by what name have you done this?"

8 Then Peter, filled with the Holy Spirit, said to them, "Rulers of the people and elders of Israel. . . .

10 "let it be known to you all, and to all the people of Israel, that by the name of Jesus Christ of Nazareth, whom you crucified, whom God raised from the dead, by Him this man stands here before you whole. . . .

14 And seeing the man who had been healed standing with them, they could say nothing against it.

15 But when they had commanded them to go aside out of the council, they conferred among themselves,

16 saying, "What shall we do to these men? For, indeed, that a notable miracle has been done through them is evident to all who dwell in Jerusalem, and we cannot deny it.

17 "But so that it spreads no further among the people, let us severely threaten them, that from now on they speak to no man in this name."

18 And they called them and commanded them NOT TO SPEAK AT ALL NOR TEACH IN THE NAME OF JESUS.

The Pharisees and Sadducees were afraid that if they punished Peter and John too severely, it would start a riot among the people who witnessed the miracle. So after commanding the disciples to stop preaching in the Name of Jesus, they let them go.

Think about it! Imagine the authorities calling *you* in and ordering you, "Don't preach anymore in Jesus' Name! If you do, you are going to be in *big* trouble!" What would you do?

I'll tell you what you'd *better* do. Start praying for God's supernatural power to come on the scene! I guarantee that you'd need more than your own strength to defy the authorities of the day and stand steadfast in God.

Peter and John knew they needed more boldness than they possessed in themselves. So they immediately went to their own company of believers. They prayed for God's supernatural strength to empower them so they could boldly preach God's Word in spite of every opposing circumstance.

ACTS 4:29–30
29 "Now, Lord, look on their threats, and GRANT TO YOUR SERVANTS THAT WITH ALL BOLDNESS THEY MAY SPEAK YOUR WORD,
30 "by stretching out Your hand to heal, and THAT SIGNS AND WONDERS MAY BE DONE through the name of Your holy Servant Jesus."

As the believers prayed, the power of God came into such glorious manifestation that the very building began to shake! The believers were all empowered by the Holy Spirit, and they went forth boldly preaching the Word with signs and wonders following (Acts 4:31; 5:12). It was revival time! Thank God for the supernatural power of the Holy Spirit!

God's supernatural power is also available to you as you are obedient to fulfill your ministry. If your motives are right—if your only desire is to lift up Jesus and build the Kingdom of God—when you call upon God's power to work for you, it will remove the obstacles Satan has placed in your path. And God's power will supernaturally set people free and bring revival on the scene!

But if you only desire to receive praise from men and personal gain, God's power *won't* work for you. Like King Saul after he disobeyed the Lord, you'll eventually discover that the anointing—the power of God—has become inoperative for you.

This day in which we live is definitely not a time to get bogged down in your spiritual walk with wrong motives and desires. You don't have time to fool around with your flesh. You have a high calling to answer and an important part to play in the great revival of this hour!

judge yourself of sin

Fulfilling your part in God's plan for revival depends on whether you live a holy life from a pure heart. You won't be able to successfully answer God's call with sin in your life.

If we're going to experience true revival, we first need to *clean up our camp by repenting of sin* (Deut. 23:14). There can't be true revival until the camp is clean, and we as ministers should set the example by judging ourselves.

Repentance always precedes revival. Throughout the ages, revival was born when believers willingly humbled themselves before the Lord. Their hearts were stirred with revival fire as they sought the Lord, asking Him to mold them into vessels fit for His use in the Kingdom of God.

The Bible says judgment begins at the house of the Lord (1 Peter 4:17). If we want to succeed in fulfilling God's call on our lives, we must judge ourselves and repent of anything that isn't pleasing to God.

I didn't say we should judge our wife or husband or those around us. If we do that, we *will* be judged by the Lord (Matt. 7:1). I said we need to judge *ourselves*!

The call of God is sacred and holy, and we don't have any business fooling around with ungodly pleasures. If we really want to see revival in our midst, we need to quit rationalizing our sin and begin to live holy lives that are separate from the world.

For instance, the Bible says to shun the very appearance of evil (1 Thess. 5:22). That includes the practice of social drinking. Christians shouldn't be drinking alcohol!

I've seen Christians stumble in their spiritual walk because they watched other believers drink socially. But the Bible tells all believers *"not to put a stumbling block or a cause to fall in our brother's way"* (Rom. 14:13).

I know a woman who was once a committed Christian. One day she saw some believers sipping wine with their meal and decided she could do that too. One thing led to another, and that woman eventually became an alcoholic.

I'm telling you, some believers will answer to God for being a stumbling block to others! Yes, God is a God of mercy. But the Bible also says that God is a God Who judges sin (Heb. 10:30).

Also, believers who commit sexual sin need to repent and clean up their lives. There is no place in the Kingdom of God for sexual sins such as fornication, adultery, and homosexuality! Homosexuals who call themselves "preachers of the Gospel" are starting homosexual churches in numerous places. Some of them claim the Holy Spirit moves miraculously in their services.

But according to the Bible, there's *no way* the Spirit of God could dwell in the midst of homosexual congregations that persist in their sin. God won't violate His Word and sanction homosexuality, which the Bible calls an abomination before the Lord (Lev. 18:22; 20:13; 1 Cor. 6:9).

If you're going to fulfill God's call on your life and help bring revival on this earth, you must keep your spirit clean of *all* the world's contamination and ungodliness! You won't be able to stay spiritually clean if you're continually watching worldly movies or television programs or reading worldly books.

You won't be able to keep your mind full of the Word of God if you let filth come through your eyes and ears. You may make it to Heaven, but ungodliness will keep you out of fellowship with God, hinder your ministry, and keep you from achieving everything God has for you.

These are just a few areas where the Church needs to clean up its camp. If Christians will judge themselves, they won't be judged (1 Cor. 11:31).

If you make a mistake and sin, God isn't going to break off His relationship with you. But He'll wait to see what you do after you make the mistake. He wants you to repent and judge *yourself* and turn from your sin.

Judgment begins with the house of the Lord. It's time to clean up the camp, friend!

So get serious about dealing with sin in your life so God can use you mightily in this hour the way He wants to. Pour out your heart before God, confess your sin to Him, and He will cleanse you by the blood of Jesus (1 John 1:9). Then turn away from that sin and determine never to do it again. Let your heart continually be an open book before the Lord, so He can search your heart and deal with any area that displeases Him (Ps. 139:23–24).

It's up to you to keep all sin out of your life because sin will keep you from moving on with God. Never allow yourself to become complacent about sin in your life or complacent about the things of God. Complacency—spiritual sloth and laziness—is a deadly poison that kills revival.

complacency kills revival

If you chart the history of the Church, you'll find that God has sent revival—a fresh outpouring of the Holy Spirit—every so often throughout the centuries. God has to continually revive His people. Too often they start out on fire for the things of God and then become complacent and apathetic in their Christian walk.

For example, look at revival as it occurred in the United States in the last 150 years. In 1857, a far-reaching revival began in this country. The next year in the midst of that revival, the great evangelist D.L. Moody began his ministry. Moody didn't start the revival of 1857—the revival started Moody!

Thirty-five years later in 1893, Moody was quoted as saying, "Would to God before I die that I could see another revival like the one begun in 1857!" Moody still experienced great success in his own ministry, but he made that statement because he saw so much apathy in the Church of his day.

In his own personal life and ministry, Moody made sure he stayed "revived" and on fire for God. But he watched as many believers, ministers and laypeople alike, became complacent as the spirit of revival began to wane.

In the decades following the revival of 1857, many believers lost the fire of revival in their own hearts. Instead, they got caught up in theological arguments, became apathetic, and accomplished very little for the Lord.

Then in 1906, a new revival swept this land from coast to coast. On an unknown street named Azusa in the city of Los Angeles, a run-down building became the world center for a sovereign move of the Holy Spirit. News traveled quickly around the world that believers who had gathered in this unlikely location were receiving the gift of the Holy Spirit with the evidence of speaking in tongues.

Hundreds of spiritually hungry people journeyed to Los Angeles from all over the world to receive this supernatural gift. Many who were filled with the Holy Spirit at the Azusa Street mission then took the message of Pentecost to the ends of the earth.

People rode the tide of the Azusa Street revival for several years until that revival also began to wane. Then in the 1920s and 1930s, God raised up several other great revivalists—ministers like Smith Wigglesworth, F.F.

Bosworth, and Aimee Semple McPherson. Because these ministers were yielded vessels unto God, the supernatural power of God was mightily demonstrated through their ministries. The flame of revival burned brightly once again.

This revival lasted through the 1930s. Then World War II came, and by 1947 most of these great revivalists had died. Many believers shook their head and asked, "What are we going to do without God's generals?"

But many other believers began to seek the Lord with all their heart. They cried out to God, "Lord, we want to see the demonstration of Your supernatural power in *our* generation! We don't just want to hear about the miracles of the old days. We want a revival *now*!"

My father was one of those believers who prayed for revival at that time. As a four-year-old boy, I remember listening to Dad talk about praying for revival. Dad said that his heart was so burdened for revival, sometimes he'd wake up in the middle of the night and find himself on his knees praying in the living room, and he wouldn't know how he got there!

In 1947, the prayers of believers were answered. A great healing revival swept the nation that lasted from 1947 to 1958. Healing evangelists by the hundreds traversed this land, and many thousands of people were healed and set free by the supernatural power of God.

Then in the late 1950s, the healing revival began to wane. Only a few years later, another revival began, which we called the Charismatic Movement.

During this revival, the fire of the Holy Ghost moved into traditional churches, and thousands of denominational believers received the baptism of the Holy Spirit. The Charismatic renewal peaked in the mid-1970s, and then the fire of that revival began to die down too.

Then in the 1970s, a Word revival came on the heels of the Charismatic renewal. Churches everywhere exploded in growth as people started getting hold of the truth of faith in God's Word and their rights and privileges in Jesus Christ.

In the 1980s, the Word revival reached its peak, and it seemed many so-called "Word" people began losing their excitement about the Word of God. Their hunger to learn more about the things of God died down, and they became complacent, thinking, *I don't need to hear that. I've heard it before.*

But none of us is so spiritually mature that we don't need to be reminded of the basic truths of God's Word. It's time to shake off complacency and stir up our hunger for the move of God on this earth! Only then will we be effective ministers in God's plan for these last days.

requirements for revival

As you obey God's call to the ministry, you don't want to struggle and strain just to bear little or no fruit for the Lord, do you? You want to reap an *abundant* harvest of souls for God's Kingdom! That's what revival is all about!

But there are some requirements we must fulfill to see revival explode in our generation. First, we must be *spiritually hungry for more of God.*

Today we are experiencing the beginning of the mightiest outpouring of the Holy Spirit the world has ever seen. Now as never before, we need to allow God to reach down by the Holy Spirit and stir up the embers of revival in our hearts. We are called of God to the ministry, and our heart cry should be nothing less than *worldwide revival!*

Just as a blacksmith's bellows fan the coals of his fire, we need the wind of the Holy Spirit to blow mightily on the coals of our hearts. We must let God stir us until the flame of revival blazes strongly and ignites a supernatural move of God throughout the earth!

Revival comes when the Church is hungry to see souls won into God's Kingdom. It comes when both ministers and laypeople alike dare to pay the price to seek the Lord the way great men and women of God have done in times past.

Believers who experienced former revivals tasted some of the glory which is yet to be revealed to us. And they were faithful to pass on to us the vision—the torch of revival which burned so deeply in their hearts.

When God's flame of revival burns inside us, we won't be content to sit around and do nothing for the Lord. We'll want to get up and answer our call. We'll eagerly take our part in the move of God's Spirit on the earth.

We won't be concerned with praying for just our own needs to be met. Our hearts will burn with the desire to pray for others and minister to their needs.

But before we experience a spiritual awakening, we must learn to *pray through* as we ask God for revival. We'll have to spend time praying for the lost! What does it mean to pray through? It means you pray until you experience a note of victory in your spirit concerning those you are praying for. And you reach that point of victory through persistent prayer.

If you've been a Christian very long, there have probably been times when you've prayed and it seemed as though you were just mouthing words; your prayers were bouncing off the ceiling. When that happens, don't get frustrated and quit! Keep seeking God with your whole heart.

If you'll persevere in prayer, you'll come to the place where external circumstances and natural thoughts will distract you less and less. Even ringing phones, playing children, and barking dogs won't distract you. You'll be so engrossed in the Presence of God, you won't notice.

When you enter into that dimension of prayer, it's easy to pray. You may think you've only prayed 10 minutes, but when you look at your watch, you find you've prayed for a long time!

Also, to experience revival, we must *be committed to what God has called us to do.* We must completely sell out to God, giving Him everything we are and everything we possess. That's the only way we can reach our highest potential in the ministry.

Commitment seems to be a dirty word to some believers. Some Christians have come out of the bondage of religious tradition, but they've taken their liberty in Christ to an extreme by refusing to commit themselves to anything. They would rather be a "holy floater," floating from one church to another, than settle down and commit themselves to one local church family. Their spiritual walk suffers because they don't have any roots or foundation in their lives.

But in the revival that's beginning in this hour, we must be committed to obey God and fulfill our part in God's master plan. We should be willing to say, "Lord, I'll obey

Your call. I'll preach, witness, or help behind the scenes. I'll do whatever *You* want me to do."

Some ministers want revival so they can be in the limelight and enjoy a great place of prominence where everyone knows who they are. But I'll tell you something. I've reached the point where I want to see God move, whether or not I'm ever a part of it! If the Spirit of God manifests Himself through another preacher, I don't feel the least bit jealous. I just rejoice because God is moving!

Let's not be jealous of one another. It's a sad thing to see preachers who are jealous of one another, and it hinders the manifestations of the Holy Spirit in our midst. Let's rejoice together in our united commitment to usher in the move of God's Spirit on this earth!

I realize the seriousness of the day we live in. But I also realize that the supernatural power of God is far greater than the power of the devil. The devil's strategies can be thwarted as believers commit themselves to bringing revival to this land.

Revival is the cry of the hour. Don't fail to take *your* place in this last-days revival. Answer your call!

If you don't take your place in God's plan for these last days, it's not God's fault. It's yours, because failures are man-made. Successes are God-made. God's supernatural power is at your disposal by the Word of God and the Holy Spirit to make you a success in your life and ministry.

So determine to be the success God intends you to be. Allow the wind of the Holy Spirit to blow through your heart and cause the desire for revival to burn brightly.

Always depend on God's supernatural power as you answer His call. Don't ever try to bring about revival in your own strength. Stand strong for truth in the midst of the world's ungodliness and boldly speak God's Word, with signs and wonders following.

Determine *to do* the greater works of Jesus and not just *to talk* about them. As you make revival the cry of your heart and stir yourself up to move with God, the supernatural power of God will flow through you to set people free!

times of preparation

preparing
for the ministry

throughout the Bible, it's clear that *God trains and prepares those whom He calls*. For instance, in the Old Testament Joshua was trained under Moses' ministry (Exod. 33:11; Deut. 34:9). The prophet Samuel traveled in circuit to several towns in Israel, training young men who were called as prophets (1 Sam. 7:16; 19:20). And Elisha was trained in the ministry as he assisted the prophet Elijah (2 Kings 3:11).

Even the Apostle Paul went through a training period. After being filled with the Holy Spirit, he didn't come out of the house on Straight Street and immediately begin his ministry. The Bible says he first spent a period of time in the Arabian desert and in Damascus (Gal. 1:16–17). During that time, God evidently began to train Paul for what He had called him to do.

GOD alone calls and anoints ministers

Training is a part of God's program for ministry. A minister should never stop training, because each new stage in his ministry requires preparation.

However, it's important to understand that *training in itself doesn't make anyone a minister*. The call to the ministry doesn't come just because one day a person decides, "I'm going to train to be a preacher."

Certainly a person can make the decision to go to Bible school and train for the ministry. But Bible school training alone doesn't automatically make a person a minister.

Before a person can ever become a true minister of the Gospel, he must be *called* by God and *anointed* by the Holy Spirit. If a person is truly called by God and obedient to prepare himself for the ministry, the time will come when the anointing of the Holy Spirit will rest upon him. That anointing will equip and empower him to fulfill the divine call of God upon him.

Unfortunately, there are many people in the ministry today whom God never called. You can tell God didn't call them because even though they may have graduated from Bible school, there's no anointing on them to preach or teach the Word.

So before you ever start preparing for the ministry, make sure that it is *God's* plan for you, and not just your own idea. Then get the difference clear in your own mind between God's responsibility and yours. God *calls and anoints* you for service. Your part is *to obey* His call.

Also, you can't put yourself in the ministry. God will train and prepare you. Then when He considers you ready, He will put you in the ministry.

Meanwhile, just be faithful to do what you know to do according to the Word of God and the leading of the Holy Spirit. Willingly obey the Lord in the times of preparation, no matter how lowly the task He gives you may seem.

That's all part of answering the call.

don't hold back!

Some people who are called to the ministry hang back and resist answering God's call. It's as if they just want to stick their toe in the "stream" of the Holy Spirit—God's call on their lives—to see if the water is warm or cold.

They toy around with the thought of entering the ministry, but they're afraid to jump into God's call. They hesitate about making the quality decision to completely commit themselves.

However, I've found that the best way to get into cold water is to get a running start and jump right into it. Once you jump, you can't change your mind in mid-air! You've committed yourself to getting wet!

People who have been playing around with the call of God on their lives need to just take off, start running, and jump into God's perfect will. They need to make the decision, "God, I don't care what it takes or what I have to give up—I'm answering Your call!"

If you've been holding back from fully committing yourself to God's call, the Lord could be saying to you, "You've followed your own plan long enough. Now it's time to fulfill the ministry I've planned for you. It's time to answer My call on your life!"

You see, as long as you try to ignore God's call, your life will be like a roller-coaster ride. You'll be up one day and down the next.

Although you may experience some victories, they won't be long-lasting. Victories will seem to melt away, and you'll always be struggling to stay on top of adverse circumstances.

But once you surrender to God and answer His call to the ministry, you'll experience a deep sense of peace and joy. There's such contentment in knowing you've begun the journey to do what God has called you to do!

If you're in the center of God's will, your peace and contentment will remain unshaken no matter what's going on around you or how impossible circumstances look in the natural. But it's only by obeying God's call that you'll ever find this kind of peace and joy.

That doesn't mean you won't experience mixed emotions as you begin your journey of preparation for the ministry. Anyone who faces new and unknown challenges as he or she follows God will experience some mixed emotions. Change in life is not always easy.

For example, when you walk with God and do what He asks you to do, you may have to let go of your natural "security blankets." You may have to walk away from the security of a job or of relatives and friends.

But your only other option is to become stagnant in your spiritual walk and never fulfill God's purpose for your life. That's what happens when you aren't willing to take the first step and begin your journey into the unknown—your preparation and training for the ministry.

The road God wants you to travel lies before you. It's your choice to either sit down and stagnate or walk down that road toward fulfilling your destiny—the ministry God has called *you* to.

As you begin your journey, you'll have to keep trusting the Lord, knowing He will never fail you. Be assured that no matter what changes you have to go through or what you have to give up to serve Him, nothing can compare to the blessings you'll receive because you obeyed His call.

I'm not telling you that preparing for the ministry is easy. But I will tell you this: As long as you obey God, He'll never let you down. Since the day God placed the first man, Adam, on this earth until this very hour, God has *never* failed. He's never let anyone down yet, and He's not going to start with you!

GOD gives second chances!

Perhaps you tried to answer the call of God in times past. But because you made some mistakes and experienced some failures, you gave up. If that's the case, God will give you another opportunity to fulfill your call to the ministry.

John Mark is a biblical example of a person who received a second chance to fulfill his call. For reasons unknown to us, John Mark left Paul and Barnabas in the middle of their first missionary journey (Acts 13:13).

Barnabas later wanted to take Mark with them on their second missionary journey. But Paul disagreed; he didn't want Mark to go because he'd left them prematurely on the first journey. So in essence, Paul told Barnabas, "All right, if you want to take Mark, go ahead. I'll take Silas and follow a different route" (Acts 15:37–40).

But in the following years, John Mark proved himself faithful to Paul, and Paul gave him another chance. Paul later wrote Timothy, "*. . . Get Mark and bring him with you, FOR HE IS USEFUL TO ME FOR MINISTRY*" (2 Tim. 4:11).

Paul wouldn't have said that to Timothy if Mark hadn't been doing something right! Evidently, Mark had proved himself, earned a good reputation, and become an asset to Paul.

Although Mark failed in his first endeavor on the mission field, he didn't make the same mistake twice. He made the best of his second chance. He proved himself to be profitable for the ministry, and he later wrote one of the four Gospels. Let that encourage you!

If you made mistakes in the past when you tried to answer the call of God, it's time to let go of those failures. God wants to give you a second chance, so don't let the past hound you and keep you from doing what God wants you to do right now. Make the decision to let the mistakes of the past be just that—in the past, covered by the blood of Jesus. Refuse to let those past mistakes defeat you.

I once read a letter from a minister who had allowed the devil to pull him into error, and it almost ruined his ministry. But he repented and asked the Lord to forgive him. When he wrote this letter to me, he was attempting to get his life and ministry back on track.

Even though this minister had repented, the devil harassed him mentally with accusing thoughts. The devil kept telling him, *You really messed up! Now you'll never make it in the ministry.* The minister had listened to the devil's lies so much that he wondered if he was going insane.

I talked to this minister at length about Satan's strategies in his life. I explained to him that it wasn't God who was accusing and condemning him because Satan, not God, is the accuser of the brethren (Rev. 12:10). This minister was set free from guilt and condemnation and went on to fulfill his ministry.

Don't let guilt and condemnation defeat *you*! Don't let the devil keep you from answering God's call by accusing you of past mistakes that are covered by the blood of Jesus. Take authority over him in the Name of Jesus! Renew your mind daily with the Word of God and allow the Holy Spirit to be the Helper He wants to be in you.

The past doesn't have to hinder you from doing what God has called you to do. If you'll depend on the Helper inside you and renew your mind with the Word of God, He'll help you overcome any guilt and condemnation from past mistakes. The Holy Spirit will enable and equip you to go forth and succeed no matter what mistakes you've made. Then, like John Mark, you, too, can prove yourself to be profitable for the ministry!

run to win!

When you answer the call on your life, you should have every intention of succeeding. Don't even entertain the thought of quitting or failing in the ministry. As the Bible says, "Run your spiritual race *to win*" (1 Cor. 9:24)!

In a real race, usually only one runner gets the first-place prize. But in our spiritual race, God has set before each one of us a separate race to run (Heb. 12:1). Therefore, if we finish our course and fulfill God's purpose for our life, we'll each receive a crown (Acts 20:24; 1 Cor. 9:25; 2 Tim. 4:8).

Running your course in the ministry is a different kind of spiritual race than you've ever run before. If you want to succeed in this race, you *can't* have the attitude, *It doesn't matter whether I win or lose; it's how I play the game.* It *does* matter whether you win or lose in your spiritual race! Winning—finishing your course in victory—is what it's all about.

Personally, I never do anything just to do it. Whatever I do for the Lord, I put my whole heart into accomplishing it to the best of my ability because I want to succeed.

Starting when I was a young boy, my dad taught me, "Anything worth doing is worth doing right. If something isn't worth giving everything you've got to, then don't do it at all." I live my life by that principle. Everything I do—preach, pray, play sports, or whatever it is—I do with every ounce of energy I possess.

Don't be satisfied sitting on the sidelines watching others win *their* race. And don't be content to come in second place in your race. Run *your* race to win!

I'll give you an illustration from my own life to show you the attitude you need to succeed in the ministry.

When I was running track as a teenager, I made up my mind I was going to be the best runner I could be. I went to practice every afternoon. After the team finished running laps, I'd stay out and run several extra laps by myself. Sometimes on Saturday when we didn't have practice, I'd go to the field and spend an hour or more running the track.

The extra work paid off later at the state track meet. I was on the team for the 880-yard relay race—what today is the 800-meter relay. When it was my turn to run, I ran with all my might. Because I had trained hard, I was able to reach down on the inside of myself and draw on the added strength I had built up through extra practice. I pushed myself beyond what I thought was my limit. I kept telling myself, *I cannot be defeated, and I will not quit!*

That extra strength gave me the opportunity to help move our team into first place. Many times in my life, my decision to do my best and work hard to win has made the difference between failure and success.

throw off all the weights

No one has ever broken a world record or won an Olympic medal without training properly beforehand.

The same is true in the spiritual realm. Before you can fulfill your ministry and win your spiritual race, you need to lay aside all the weights and sins which would hinder you from training properly.

HEBREWS 12:1

1 Therefore we also, since we are surrounded by so great a cloud of witnesses, LET US LAY ASIDE EVERY WEIGHT, AND THE SIN WHICH SO EASILY ENSNARES US, and let us run with endurance the race that is set before us.

Look at the way boxers train for a match. Why do you think they retreat to a training camp and get away from their familiar surroundings and from every distraction? They deliberately lay aside all weights. They separate themselves from anything that would distract them or hinder them from taking the time to get into top condition.

The same is true for other professional athletes. For example, many times at training camps, the athletes have a 10 o'clock curfew. If anyone is caught out of the dormitory after curfew, he has to pay a big fine. The trainers impose those rules because they know athletes can't prepare properly for the season unless they separate themselves from every distraction.

To be successful in your life and ministry, at times you'll have to separate yourself from distractions too, and just focus on the Lord. And you'll need to stay alert to recognize weights that would slow you down in your spiritual race. As soon as you see anything in your life that hinders you from following God with your whole heart, throw that weight off!

When I was running track and was getting ready for a race, I made sure I put on the lightest shoes and the most lightweight track uniform I could find. I sure didn't wear my baseball cleats and overcoat! I didn't want anything to slow me down and keep me from winning the race.

So don't let anyone or anything distract or hinder you, weigh you down, or trip you up as you run the race set before you! You've begun to run your spiritual race, and you *will* succeed in finishing your course as you train properly and run faithfully according to the Word of God.

a diamond in the rough

Once you begin to prepare for the ministry, you'll find God's training program isn't always easy. You see, in God's eyes you're like an uncut diamond that needs to be meticulously fashioned and polished into a precious stone. If you're ever going to become the able minister God has called you to be, He has to cut the rough edges of carnality and spiritual immaturity off your life.

A diamond in the rough looks just like any other common rock. There isn't anything pretty about it. But inside that ordinary-looking rock is the possibility of a beautiful jewel.

If an untrained person took a hammer and started chiseling away at that stone, it would end up looking like nothing more than a *broken* rock. What could have been a very expensive gem would be worthless because someone tried to cut it who didn't know what he was doing.

But imagine a master diamond cutter taking that ordinary-looking rock and carefully removing the drab, rough edges with his special tools. When the master diamond cutter finishes shaping what once looked like a common rock, he holds in his hand a brilliant, precious jewel.

God is the great Master Diamond Cutter. During your preparation for the ministry, He wants to smooth off your rough edges and polish you so you shine like a priceless gem to His glory.

God's cutting process can sometimes seem difficult. As He gradually removes those things in your life that would hinder you in the ministry, such as selfishness and worldly pursuits, your flesh can complain.

The Lord will also polish you, making those areas of past defeat shine with victory. Polishing a rough diamond requires friction and produces heat. In the same way, the polishing process in your life will sometimes seem hot and uncomfortable. But you can be sure that God is always at work to benefit you—not to harm you.

So yield your life to the expert workmanship of the Master. When pressures come during your preparation, let God use those times of stress to fashion and polish you into a brilliant jewel for His service.

timing is important

Timing is an important part of successfully answering God's call. Do you know you can be in the *right* place at the *wrong* time and end up struggling to fulfill your ministry?

I've known people who missed God's timing in answering their call. Sometimes they missed God's perfect timing because they weren't willing to lose the guarantee of financial security. Instead of seeking God for *His* timing, they waited to answer the call until *they* wanted to go.

We noticed, however, that those who did what they wanted to do at the expense of responding to God's timing never really amounted to anything in the ministry. They answered their call on *their* terms instead of on *God's* terms.

Moving in God's timing is important because it affects not only your life but the lives of others. Why is that? Because people all over the world are hurting and in need. If you don't reach them when they need you, it's possible you could get there too late to help them. That's happened before.

For example, I once read a missionary's account of what happened when he arrived at a certain village in Africa. The tribal chief of this village had gotten saved years before, but he didn't know enough of the Word to tell the rest of his tribe how to get born again. So he began to pray that the Lord would send someone who could lead his tribe to Him.

As that tribal chief prayed, the Lord gave him a vision. In the vision, a man came to the village and preached the Gospel, and many of the villagers were born again.

After the chief received that vision, years passed. Finally the missionary whom this chief had seen in the vision arrived at the village. The first words out of the chief's mouth were, "We've been waiting for you. You are the one I saw in a vision many years ago. But what took you so long? Many in my tribe have died without ever knowing Jesus. Why did you take so long to come?"

This missionary had to get on his face before God and repent, because he'd hung back and taken his time about answering God's call on his life. He could have come earlier, but he decided to do some other things first. He wanted to make sure every detail in the natural looked right before he moved out on the mission field. But he missed God's timing, and as a result other people suffered the consequences.

The missionary said that as he repented before God, the words of the tribal chief kept ringing in his ears: "What took you so long? What took you so long?"

Friend, the hearts of desperate people everywhere are crying out for help. The end of this age is near. Seek the Lord diligently to know His timing for you to move out into the ministry. May it never be said of you, "What took you so long?"

Answering God's call and preparing for the ministry is truly a journey of faith; but seeking God for His timing is also important. So put your faith solidly in the Lord. Make up your mind that, together, God and you make a team.

With the Word of God and the Holy Spirit within to help and guide you, nothing has to keep you from succeeding in the ministry. You *can* finish your course with joy and fulfill your call!

servant
or mercenary?

every person who is called to the ministry must determine if he is entering the ministry as a true servant of the Lord, or as a mercenary—one who serves for impure motives and personal gain.

What are *your* motives for going into the ministry? Do you have a heart to serve people? Does your heart break when you see people in desperate need or in bondage to the devil? Is your vision for ministry to reach out to others to set them free by the truth of the Gospel? Or are your thoughts focused on building a big name, a big ministry, and fame and fortune for yourself?

Answering these questions will help you evaluate your motives for going into the ministry. If you're going to please God, it's important to make sure your motives are pure before you ever answer God's call. And personal checkups on your motives should continue throughout your life and ministry.

Are you entering the ministry as a *servant* or as a *mercenary*? What do I mean by that? According to *Vine's Expository Dictionary of Biblical Words*, the Greek word *doulos* translated *servant* in the Bible, means "subjection without the idea of bondage."[1]

One dictionary meaning of the word *servant* is "a person who helps or assists another." The word *servant* carries the meaning of someone who has a humble and submissive attitude in the service they perform for others.

On the other hand, the word *mercenary* means "a person who acts or works for payment only." In other words, a mercenary's motive for entering the ministry is personal gain, not the benefit of others.

What do your thoughts center on when you think about the ministry? Are they about you?

Your focus largely determines whether you have the heart of a servant or the heart of a mercenary. So evaluate what you give most of your time and attention to in your thought life. Examine what most of your prayers and petitions to the Lord focus on when you talk to Him about the ministry.

Then honestly ask yourself, *What is most important to me as I answer God's call to the ministry?* Is it your own promotion? Are you just interested in obtaining a new car, house, airplane, or beautiful new ministry building? Or is your main reason for entering the ministry to see people delivered from the bondage of Satan, sin, and sickness?

If your main reason for going into the ministry is to build a big ministry and make a great name for yourself in Christian circles, your motives are wrong. Your motives for answering the call to the ministry should always be *to set the captives free and to help build the Kingdom of God.*

I'm not saying it's wrong to believe for your own personal needs and for the practical needs of your ministry to be met. But make sure the driving force of your life is to be a servant of Jesus Christ. Make sure you want to be equipped with the supernatural power of God so you can rescue people out of bondage and bring them into God's glorious Kingdom of eternal life. Make it your constant ambition to proclaim the Gospel, heal the sick, and set at liberty those held captive in Satan's grip!

servants, not slaves

Ministers don't become servants because God forces them to serve Him. God doesn't call *slaves* to the ministry. No, ministers of the Gospel become willing *bondservants* of the Lord.

A bondservant is one who voluntarily *chooses* to be the Lord's servant because God *asks* him to follow Jesus' example. In the example Jesus set for us, He humbled Himself and came to earth to serve mankind.

PHILIPPIANS 2:5–8
5 Let this mind be in you which was also in CHRIST JESUS,
6 who, being in the form of God, did not consider it robbery to be equal with God,
7 but made Himself of no reputation, TAKING THE FORM OF A BONDSERVANT, and coming in the likeness of men.
8 And being found in appearance as a man, HE HUMBLED HIMSELF and became obedient to the point of death, even the death of the cross.

Jesus' purpose for coming to earth was to serve mankind. Throughout His earthly ministry, Jesus ministered to the needs of people. But His servant's heart was best demonstrated when He willingly went to the Cross to redeem mankind through His death, burial, and resurrection.

Jesus, the Good Shepherd, gave His life willingly for His sheep (John 10:11). The only way we can represent Jesus to the world is to be like Him. That means we must give ourselves freely to minister to others from a servant's heart.

The Apostle Paul also showed us an example of a willing servant of God by his life of self-sacrifice for others: *"For though I am free from all men, I HAVE MADE MYSELF A SERVANT TO ALL, THAT I MIGHT WIN THE MORE"* (1 Cor. 9:19).

Notice, however, that being a servant didn't mean Paul had to try to please people at the expense of obeying God.

GALATIANS 1:10
10 For do I now persuade men, or God? Or do I seek to please men? For if I still pleased men, I would not be A BONDSERVANT OF CHRIST.

In this verse, in essence, Paul said, "I seek to please the One Who called me to be a servant—not people who try to pressure me to do things their way." Yes, Paul had a servant's heart and ministered to the needs of people. But he was a *God-pleaser*, not a *man-pleaser*.

You see, as ministers, we are supposed to serve people. But we are *not* supposed to try to satisfy people's carnal opinions about what we should be doing in the ministry. First and foremost, we must be sure we serve *God*.

EPHESIANS 6:6
6 not with eyeservice, as men-pleasers, but as bondservants of Christ, doing the will of God FROM THE HEART.

That brings up another important point. You can't be an effective servant unless you do the will of God from your heart. So be certain you do God's will from a willing *heart*, not from your *head* out of a sense of duty. There's a big difference between the two.

You see, it's possible for you to harbor an unwilling attitude in your heart even though you are obeying what God told you to do. In fact, when your attitude is wrong, you're more of a *slave* than a *servant* of God, and God doesn't want unwilling slaves. And if you're doing the will of God from your head instead of your heart, you'll struggle in the ministry.

But when you willingly serve God from your heart, you're not only *obedient*, you're also a *willing* servant of Jesus Christ. The Bible says the willing *and* obedient eat the good of the land and are blessed (Isa. 1:19).

ministers who are mercenaries

Sad to say, many people who call themselves ministers are *not* servants. Their main motive in the ministry is to gain fame and fortune, *not* to serve people from a pure heart.

Too many who are called to the ministry have forgotten what it is to care about others. Instead, they're consumed with visions of big ministries, complete with personal glory, power, prestige, and the comforts of life.

For instance, some ministers want to become big-name preachers like Smith Wigglesworth or Kathryn Kuhlman. They want to be famous to lift up their own name rather than to minister to people's needs. That shows a mercenary's heart, not a servant's heart.

When I say that, I know I'm bringing a strong indictment against some ministers. But we need to stand up for the truth so that humble servants of God—*not* self-seeking mercenaries—can be raised up to build God's Kingdom on the earth in these last days.

Instead of *seeking to minister*, mercenaries spend their energy *seeking a ministry*. In other words, they are seeking a name for themselves. The difference between those two goals—helping others versus selfish ambition—needs to be forever stamped on your heart as you endeavor to answer the call of God on your life.

Someone who seeks a *ministry* looks for big crowds. *Numbers*, not *people*, are all-important to him. The mercenary's idea of a successful ministry is big meetings in big convention centers. This kind of minister usually wants to drive up to the meeting at the last minute in a fancy car, strut around on the platform as he preaches, and then slip out the back door at the end of the service without ministering to anyone.

On the other hand, a servant who seeks *to minister to* others sees people who are bound by sin or sickness—people who need *Jesus*—and his heart of love and compassion is deeply stirred for them. He doesn't think about his own personal gain and convenience. All he wants to do is reach out and help hurting people so they can be set free by the power of God.

Of course I realize that different kinds of services sometimes require different methods of ministry. For example, in the evangelistic ministry, at times the crowd is so huge it's difficult to minister personally to individuals.

But a true minister will always keep the needs of the people uppermost in his mind. He'll seek God so he will know the best way to minister effectively to the people in each meeting.

On the other hand, a mercenary isn't interested in ministering effectively to the people. He just has the attitude, *Look at me! This is MY ministry!* But it isn't his ministry at all. He would find that out quickly enough if he ever tried to heal the sick or get people saved in his own strength! No one can do *anything* of eternal value without the power of God working through him.

So get it clear in your mind that *you* don't have a ministry—Jesus does. You have been entrusted with *the Lord's* ministry, and you have a responsibility to faithfully carry it out.

As I heard one minister say, "Let go of *your* ministry so you can do *the work of Jesus Christ.*" You have been called to serve *God* and others, not to serve *yourself.* And as you depend on His power to equip you, He will work through you to minister to others.

servants don't wait for 'the big break'

Since a mercenary is in the ministry for selfish ambition, he makes ministerial decisions based on impure motives just for personal gain.

I've seen some believers who are called to the ministry just sit around and never accomplish anything for God because they are always looking for "the big break." They're looking for a ministerial opportunity that suits *their* personal desires and selfish ambitions.

For instance, a minister with the heart of a mercenary wouldn't even consider ministering in small churches. If he heard about a few people in a small town who were looking for a pastor to come and start a church, he probably wouldn't even pray about it or consider it. He'd just say, "Oh, I believe the Lord has more for me than *that*."

Even though he may be inexperienced in the ministry, the mercenary wants a ministerial position that offers status and financial security, such as pastoring a big, established church.

A person like that isn't thinking about ministering to *people*. His goal is to make things comfortable for *himself*. And because his motives are wrong, if he ever did get a position like that, he'd make a mess of it.

When a mercenary considers ministerial opportunities, he thinks, *What's in this for me?* Often a mercenary wants the promise of a certain amount of money before he will accept an invitation to preach. Or he wants the promise of having a leadership position. He is more concerned with his own gain than he is with determining the will of God in the matter.

I remember one young, inexperienced minister who was just starting out in the ministry and didn't have anywhere to preach. I was standing nearby when a pastor asked him to come and preach at his church. The minister responded, "Well, I'll pray about it, Brother, and get back to you."

When I heard him say that, I thought, *Why didn't he just accept that invitation to preach? I happen to know he doesn't have any place to preach for the next six months!*

So later I asked this young minister why he didn't accept the invitation. He told me, "Well, it's just a little country church. It would actually cost me money to travel there to preach."

When he said that, I realized why he didn't have anywhere to preach for the next six months. He wasn't willing to go wherever God opened a door of opportunity! That man didn't have a servant's heart. He was more concerned about what benefit *he* would get from preaching than he was about ministering to the needs of *people*.

An attitude like that is totally unscriptural. Anyone who is called to the ministry must be ready to go *wherever* the Lord leads him, regardless of how insignificant or undesirable the Lord's assignment may seem to him.

As I was growing up, my dad always set a good example as the Lord's servant. For instance, in 1950, the pastor of a tiny country church in Louisiana asked Dad to come and preach for him.

Dad was already well-known in Pentecostal circles and had many invitations to preach in some of the largest churches in the nation. But Dad had a servant's heart, and he preached wherever the Lord told him to go.

Dad sensed the Lord leading him to preach in this small country church, so he agreed to go and minister there. After Dad accepted that preaching invitation, the devil tried to bombard his mind with thoughts of doubt and unbelief, telling him, *You can't get the offerings you need to live on from a little church like that!* But Dad wouldn't listen. He just said, "I'm going to obey God and serve the people."

Dad finished the meetings he was holding in a large church in another state, and traveled down to Louisiana to begin meetings in this little country church. The pastor and his wife welcomed him into their modest home. These simple folks had only a coal-oil stove and "a path and a house"—an outhouse—instead of an indoor bathroom.

Dad held meetings for three weeks in that little church, and many people's lives were changed as they sat under the teaching of God's Word. And as it turned out, Dad received more in offerings in that small country church than he had in the large church where he'd just preached!

Obeying God from a servant's heart always brings reward. I discovered the truth of that statement when I started out in the ministry. Once my wife and I preached at a tiny church in a small Alabama town. At the time, Lynette was expecting our second child and we were believing God for $300 to help pay the hospital bill. In those early days of ministry, that was a lot of money to receive by faith.

The first evening I preached to an audience of 20 people. When I looked out and saw the small crowd, in my natural mind I thought, *I'd better change what I'm believing for! We won't be able to receive the amount of money we need from only 20 people!* But my wife and I held fast to our faith in God that our needs would be met, and we concentrated on ministering to the people, regardless of what the circumstances looked like.

Even fewer people came to the next two services. In the natural, the possibility of receiving $300 seemed slim. But we just kept ministering God's truth to the people, and word got around that people were being blessed. By the last service, the crowd had greatly increased.

As Lynette and I were preparing to leave after the last service, a man walked up to me and gave me a check. The pastor also gave us the church offering. When we got into our car, we looked at the total of these offerings. We received exactly what we'd been believing God for!

The point I'm trying to get across to you is that if you're willing to obey God, and if you concentrate on serving people, you won't have to worry about your own needs being met. As you faithfully serve people, God will take care of you.

You should always minister with the idea of benefiting others. When you minister to people from a servant's heart of love and genuine concern, your ministry *will* increase. Whether you preach to large crowds or minister behind the scenes, you can know one thing for sure: God faithfully rewards those who minister from a servant's pure heart.

be willing to be inconvenienced for the gospel

Jesus, the Head of the Church, calls us to be His representatives on this earth. To be Jesus' representatives, we must minister selflessly just as He did during His earthly ministry.

What *Jesus* personally wanted or needed didn't occupy His thoughts. Instead, He was always concerned about what *people* needed. He came to earth to minister to people, not to be ministered to by others.

In our own lives, we choose every day either to live according to our flesh or to walk in the Spirit. When we live according to our flesh, it's easy to be selfish with our time. If we're carnal, we want to do what *we* want to do when *we* want to do it.

But as ministers of the Gospel, we must live according to the Spirit of God and strive to be like Jesus. We are servants of Christ, and we need to be willing to be inconvenienced for the sake of the Gospel so we can serve people.

Personal inconvenience in the ministry is sometimes a part of serving God faithfully, regardless of the cost. I know. I grew up as the son of a preacher.

As a young boy, I remember the many times our family would sit down to dinner, only to have the phone ring. People were always needing Dad to minister to them. Anyone who grew up in a minister's home can tell you the same thing.

It's not pleasant for a minister to have to constantly leave the dinner table to go help someone and then come back to an empty table and cold food. It's not easy on the minister's family, either. That's why every member of a minister's family needs to learn to develop a servant's heart.

When someone has a serious need, you can't say, "Call me back at a more convenient time; I'm eating." You have a mercenary's heart if you're always telling people to call back when it's convenient for *you*. If a person has an immediate need, as a true servant of the Lord Jesus Christ, you should make yourself available to him, regardless of the inconvenience.

But that doesn't mean a minister can allow himself to be run ragged by people either. He'll have to set aside time to relax with his family and be sure he has personal time with the Lord—or he'll wear out his body!

Unfortunately, I know some ministers who are *not* willing to inconvenience themselves for anyone. Some pastors even refuse to get up in the middle of the night to make a hospital call when one of their church members has a medical emergency. You might say, "Well, I'm not a pastor." The principle is nevertheless the same.

When I was an associate pastor, I told the pastor, "For 30 years you've been getting up at all hours of the night to minister to the people in your congregation when they have a serious need.

"Pastor, you need a break," I said. "Why don't you put the church phone in my house? If anyone needs a pastor in the middle of the night, I'll go minister to him. I won't call you for help unless I need to." The pastor agreed, and I began taking the night calls when people in the congregation had an emergency.

Now don't think that particular pastoral responsibility is easy. It isn't. It isn't fun to be awakened at 3 o'clock in the morning out of a deep sleep by a ringing phone. It isn't fun to get out of bed, throw your clothes on, and leave the comforts of home to drive as fast as you can to the emergency room to help someone in need.

But the truth is, ministry is *not* always fun. Most of the time, ministry is spelled w-o-r-k! And yet it is also tremendously rewarding and personally challenging.

The point is, if you're a minister—a servant of the Lord—you must be willing to pray for and minister to the needs of others in their hour of difficulty, even if it's inconvenient for you. That's just part of fulfilling your responsibilities as God's servant to the people.

In that same church where I was an associate pastor, I remember one woman named Millie who was dying of lupus. Often she'd wake up in the middle of the night in great pain, and wouldn't be able to get back to sleep.

When that happened, Millie would call me, sometimes three or four times a night. I'd ask her, "Do you want me to come and pray for you, Millie?"

She'd usually tell me, "No, please just pray over the phone, Brother Ken." So I'd pray for her, and the pain would subside so she could go back to sleep again.

No, my flesh didn't enjoy being awakened three or four times a night. My son, Craig, was a baby at the time, and often we'd just get back to sleep after being up with him when the phone would ring again, and it was Millie needing prayer.

Yes, that was inconvenient for me. But it was a benefit to Millie, and because I was a servant of Christ, that's what counted to me. At times, my praying for her was the only relief from pain Millie ever got. So every time she called, I would reach into my heart and pray for her with all the compassion I had.

Someone might ask, "Why didn't Millie receive her healing?" I asked the Lord the same thing. I prayed, "Oh, God, why can't I get Millie to realize that she can be completely healed from this disease and not just receive a little temporary relief?"

But for whatever reason, no matter what I said, I was never able to get that truth across to Millie. So I ministered to her the best way I could until she went home to be with the Lord.

Some ministers would say, "I wouldn't put up with my phone ringing at all hours of the day and night!" With that kind of attitude, you'd better make sure you never become a pastor! A pastor is on call 24 hours a day, 365 days a year.

You see, people don't intend to have problems or emergencies, especially in the middle of the night. But crises happen unexpectedly, and people need a pastor to help them and minister to them.

When the church is small, you may be the only minister on staff and, therefore, the only one who is available to the people at all times. However, if your church is large, that responsibility should be shared with others.

Since 1985 I've pastored RHEMA Bible Church in Broken Arrow, Oklahoma. A member of the pastoral staff is on call at all times. We have a 24-hour phone line that any church member can call if an emergency arises.

A few years ago, my phone rang late one Saturday night. It was one of my associate pastors. He was on call at the time.

My associate pastor told me about a church member who had been taken to the hospital in serious condition. Even though it was midnight and I knew my associate would be at the hospital, I wanted to minister to the sick person and his family myself.

When I walked into the hospital room, the family members looked at me in surprise and exclaimed, "Pastor, what are you doing here?"

I told them, "I'm just taking care of my flock. As a pastor, I want to minister to you when you find yourself facing a crisis."

They protested, "But, Pastor, you need rest! You have to preach in the morning!"

I answered, "That doesn't make any difference. Right now is when you need me. I'll preach to the congregation in the morning, but right now I'm here to minister to you."

be touchable by the people

You see, you can't just be a Sunday-morning minister. What am I talking about? I'm talking about a minister being *available* and *touchable* in the ministry, even if it means some sacrifice on his part. People need a "touchable" minister—one who can identify with the people and make himself available to them.

Nowhere is this more true than in the pastoral ministry. A true pastor mixes and mingles with his people. He isn't some big celebrity who gets behind a pulpit and preaches every Sunday and then walks out the door. He makes himself available to his congregation.

I've enjoyed playing on our church softball team. Playing ball provides a good opportunity to get to know some of the men in the church, as well as their families. I thoroughly enjoy that avenue of getting acquainted with the people in my church. But that's just one avenue. Ministers need to look for ways to make themselves available to the congregation.

As you get to know other people and serve them with a humble heart, you'll be teaching them how to be servants too. Often they'll want to find ways to show their respect and appreciation by being a blessing to *you.*

It isn't always easy for the true servant to accept it when others serve him. But it's important to learn how *to be served* as well as how *to serve.* God designed the members of the Body of Christ to minister to one another.

However, be careful you don't begin *expecting* to be served. If you get upset because people aren't serving you the way you think they should, check up on your attitude!

Thoughts such as *I deserve to be treated better!* reveal the attitude of a mercenary, not a servant.

Just trust the Lord to meet your needs as you focus your attention on ministering to the needs of others. And as you fulfill the call of God on your life, never forget you are a representative of the Lord Jesus Christ. Strive to become the kind of minister Jesus was in His earth walk—touchable, available, and willing to be inconvenienced in order to serve and help people.

mercenary methods to raise finances

As you check up on your motives in the ministry, be particularly careful in dealing with finances. Every ministry must have money to operate. That's a fact of life. But there's a right way and a wrong way to obtain the finances needed to operate the ministry. Be sure your methods of raising money reflect a servant's heart, not a mercenary's heart that desires only personal gain.

The mercenary puts pressure on people to give money into his ministry. Then he lavishes money extravagantly on his own personal comforts and pleasures. Also, he often resorts to gimmicks to persuade people to give to him.

One dictionary definition of a *gimmick* is "a cunning, attention-getting ploy to gain a desired end." Using gimmicks in the ministry to raise money is a mercenary's method of getting finances. It's fine to send a CD or book to people when they give you an offering. But it's another thing altogether to devise cunning gimmicks and make promises you can't keep to entice people to give.

You need to be very careful in this area of finances. Check up on your motives for initiating new programs in your ministry. For instance, are you building a new building so you can gain more prestige for yourself? Are you printing a book to make money from the profits? Or are your decisions to expand your ministry based on fulfilling the Lord's commission of reaching more people with the truth of the Gospel (Matt. 28:19–20)?

Years before my dad ever published his first book, some of his minister friends said to him, "You ought to put your teachings into print. You could make a lot of money!"

Dad never wanted money to be his motive for publishing books, so for years he put off publishing his first book. He waited until he was absolutely sure his motives were right and he had God's timing.

Today Dad and I have more than 70 million books in print, but we've never received one penny from any of our books. That money goes back into the ministry where it can reach more people for Jesus Christ.

I'm not holding up my dad and myself as great paragons of virtue just because we haven't kept the royalties from our books. That's just a decision we both made in regard to the ministry the Lord has given us.

Legally and ethically, a person can certainly live on the profits of books he's written. But if a minister's main reason for writing books is to make money or gain fame and fortune for himself rather than to help people, then he's got a problem with impure motives.

GOD's payday will come!

Although personal gain should *never* be your motive for entering the ministry, you *can* expect God to bless you for faithfully serving Him and others. As you begin in the ministry, you may have to live without some of the creature comforts you'd like to enjoy. But as you steadfastly serve the people, payday *will* eventually come.

My dad's life is a good example of this. Back in the early days of his ministry, he preached faith when he was driving a beat-up 1937 Pontiac. Every Monday he had to work on the transmission so he could drive it for the rest of the week.

For years my family didn't have much in the way of earthly possessions. For instance, when my sister and I were in elementary school, we had to make our clothes last a long time—and we didn't have many clothes to begin with! And if we needed anything extra, such as money to go on a church-group outing, we had to use our own faith and believe God for the money.

In my own ministry, I know what it's like to look into bare kitchen cupboards when you're hungry. I know what it is to be in the ministry—to make very little money and drive a car that's almost falling apart.

But I also know what it is to receive God's rewards for faithfulness. I'll never forget the day in 1976 when my wife and I stood in our garage and cried as we looked at two brand-new cars that God provided for us through other people. We didn't owe a dime on those cars. That was just one of the many blessings God has bestowed on us as we've endeavored to faithfully obey Him in the ministry.

I guarantee that, if you'll learn to serve people, you'll be taken care of by the King of kings Himself. He will take care of you as you take care of His people.

It's wonderful when God's payday comes. But I find my main joy in the ministry by *ministering to people*, not in receiving God's blessings for myself.

What if someone said to you, "You can keep all the material and financial blessings you've received in the ministry if you promise to stop serving people"? What would *you* answer?

I know what *I* would have to answer. I'd say, "Then take away the blessings! Material blessings are worthless if I receive them at the expense of ministering eternal life to people!"

As you prepare to go into the ministry, avoid the trap of a mercenary's heart at all costs! Ministers who are mercenaries at heart may look as though they're successful in the ministry. But they won't receive any reward in Heaven for what they've gained through wrong motives.

And one day those ministers will be judged by the Head of the Church (2 Cor. 5:10). I wonder what they will say to the Master when He asks them, "Were *you* a servant to My people—or a mercenary?"

So as you endeavor to answer the call of God on your life, determine to do so with the pure motives of a faithful servant. Begin to see yourself helping people who are hurting, lost, and destined for hell.

Don't set your sights on a big ministry. Focus your vision on ministering to those who will fall over the precipice of death into a burning, eternal hell without someone's help. Preach to them and share the good news of the Gospel with them in the power of the Holy Spirit, and snatch them out of Satan's clutches.

For the rest of your life and ministry, keep the burning desire to serve people stirred up within you. Then as you go forth to fulfill your ministry, you'll put yourself in a position to be all God has called you to be—a true servant of the Lord Jesus Christ—not a self-seeking mercenary!

---

1 W.E. Vine, *An Expository Dictionary of New Testament Words*, 562, in *Vine's Expository Dictionary of Biblical Words*, W.E. Vine, Merrill F. Unger, and William White Jr. (Nashville: Thomas Nelson, 1985).

requirements for
success in the ministry

Success in the ministry doesn't come automatically just because you're called of God. You'll need to meet certain scriptural requirements if you want to be successful in fulfilling your call.

be diligent

One of the first requirements for success in the ministry is *diligence*. *Diligence* means "steady, earnest, energetic effort." You must be diligent to study and prepare yourself for the task that lies before you (1 Tim. 4:13–16; 2 Tim. 2:15).

Your task is one of eternal significance. Your job is to tell others that Jesus Christ saves, heals, delivers, and is coming again. You have an awesome responsibility before God to diligently prepare to take that message to the world. Whether you fulfill that responsibility will directly affect some people's lives for eternity.

Actually, diligence is a requirement for success in *any* area of life. You're not going to be successful with the attitude, *How little can I do to get by?*

For instance, no one ever becomes a champion athlete without diligent training. And in the business world, people who are promoted to top executive positions are usually those who diligently prepared and educated themselves for the greater responsibility of those positions.

My brother-in-law, Gary, is a good example of a person who attained success in his profession because of his diligence. At 30 years of age, Gary was president of a bank. How did that happen? Through diligent preparation and study in his chosen field.

Gary didn't become president of his own bank by putting in eight hours a day as a bank employee and then going home and spending his evenings watching television. He studied hard on his own time and earned a degree in finance as well as completing graduate studies in banking.

Also, Gary didn't stop learning once he obtained his degrees. Every night while other banking employees were having fun or relaxing, Gary continued to study the latest publications on banking and finance.

Gary's diligent study paid off. The bank executives began to notice that Gary always offered innovative ideas and insightful comments. Promotion followed promotion as Gary proved himself to be a valuable asset to the bank. Finally he became the president of his own bank. And he now heads a corporation that owns several banks.

Diligence is the key to Gary's success in the banking business. The same principle holds true in the spiritual realm. Diligent study and preparation will be one of the keys to *your* success in the ministry.

As you prepare for the ministry, a spiritual mine full of hidden treasures lies before you in God's Word.

Others can point out the various veins of gold, silver, and precious stones. They can provide you with the tools you need to mine the treasures—but they can't mine God's treasures for you.

Only *you* can mine the treasures of God's Word for yourself! You are the only one who can dig into the Word, find the promises of God, and make them a reality in your own life and ministry.

Mining isn't just picking up rocks off the ground. It takes a lot of diligent effort and hard work to dig out treasures hidden deep in the earth. It's the same thing in the spiritual realm.

It takes diligent effort and hard work to become established in God's Word and seasoned in the faith walk. It's not always easy. It not only takes diligence, it also takes determination and perseverance. In fact, if you aren't willing to work harder than you've ever worked in your life, you'll never make it in the ministry.

However, let me balance that by saying you'll also need to be diligent to plan *leisure time*. Because of the many pressures experienced in the ministry, you need time to relax and enjoy yourself. Times of both spiritual and natural refreshing provide outlets to release the pressure.

Proverbs 17:22 says, "*A merry heart does good, like medicine. . . .*" It does a person good to laugh and enjoy a good time of fellowship with other believers. It benefits him, not only physically, but mentally and spiritually.

There's a time to work and a time to play (Eccl. 3:1). You *can* maintain a strong spiritual walk with the Lord and still enjoy times of relaxation. So be diligent to stay balanced in both work and leisure time as you prepare to enter the ministry.

be diligent to finish your preparation time

It's important to be diligent not only in preparation for the ministry but *to finish* your time of preparation. Otherwise, you could become just another spiritual casualty who has fallen by the wayside.

Too many people enter active ministry with only "half a load." In other words, they get only part of the message and some of the spiritual training and maturity God wants to instill in them, and then they jump into the ministry prematurely.

Because they're not fully equipped, they're ill-prepared for the demands of the ministry. Many times they get discouraged and quit, or they receive just enough knowledge to be dangerous! And because they aren't established in the Word and in godly character, they go out and cause problems in churches, wreaking havoc in the Body of Christ.

This hurting world doesn't need ill-prepared ministers who cause problems because they're still carnal and spiritually ignorant! The world doesn't need ministers who get off into error and become religious charlatans, using the ministry as a means of personal profit rather than as an avenue to help hurting people.

So be sure you don't launch into active ministry prematurely. There are no shortcuts in God's training program. It's the same way in the natural realm. There aren't any shortcuts when it comes to learning anything worthwhile.

For instance, years ago when our ministry first acquired an airplane, I learned there are no shortcuts to flying a plane safely. An important part of any pilot's training is to learn to follow flight safety rules precisely.

One of our RHEMA instructors was our ministry pilot. This man had many years of experience as both an Air Force and a private pilot. In all his years of flying, he'd never been involved in an accident. One reason he had such an excellent safety record was that he never took shortcuts in his systematic pre-flight checklist.

I flew with our pilot on many occasions. I watched him every time we prepared for takeoff. Slowly and deliberately, he would check everything on the airplane, from the wheels to the oil to the fuel.

We never started rolling down the runway until he had completed his thorough pre-flight checklist. He always complied with good safety practices as he'd been trained to do.

Pilots who take safety shortcuts when they fly set themselves up for disaster. For example, I knew a successful young businessman who took a safety shortcut one time when he was flying his twin-engine airplane.

This young businessman called the airport and told the mechanics, "Please get my plane ready. I'm flying some people to San Francisco for lunch."

When the businessman arrived at the airport, he just assumed his request had been carried out. He didn't go through the pre-flight checklist that every pilot is required to complete whenever he flies. He and his friends just climbed into the airplane and quickly headed down the runway.

Unknown to this businessman, the mechanics hadn't had time to refuel the plane before he arrived. So as soon as the airplane cleared the runway, the engines sputtered and died. The plane crashed, killing everyone on board.

Because this man had been in a hurry, he'd gotten careless and ignored flight-safety precautions. That decision cost him and his friends their lives.

In the same way, you can cause great harm in your life and ministry by trying to take shortcuts in your ministerial preparation. That's one reason why you should not try to enter the ministry before you're prepared. You see, the devil knows how to open doors that may look good, but could take you out of the will of God for your life.

Some RHEMA Bible Training Center students have made the mistake of leaving their place of preparation prematurely. When they first arrived at RHEMA, they said, "I *know* God called me here." But then we'd receive letters from the same students after Christmas break saying, "I won't be back for the rest of the school year. A door has opened for ministry, and I'm going to accept the position."

If God calls a person to a two-year ministerial training program, He doesn't want him to run off and get into active ministry after four months! That isn't the way God works! God wants people to diligently prepare themselves so they can be spiritually equipped when they enter the ministry.

At the Bible college I attended as a young man, I saw many students make that same mistake and leave their training prematurely. Some students would finish one year and quit, saying, "I can't wait. I have to go preach!"

Some of those people would hold a few meetings, and for a while they seemed to be doing well in the ministry. But when the going got rough, they weren't seasoned enough in their faith walk to stand fast on God's Word, and it wasn't long before their ministries fizzled out. The last I heard of some of those people, they had quit the ministry and were working at secular jobs.

But if it was God's will that those people train for the ministry, it was also God's will that they finish what they started! God didn't change His mind all of a sudden about His plan for their lives. When they decided not to finish their training, they got out of the will of God. That's why things didn't work right for them.

You know, we don't have time to waste making mistakes like that about the call of God. The devil is afflicting too many people who need to be set free by the power of God's Word for ministers of the Gospel to take costly detours.

The world is full of people who are bruised and confused by the devil's strategies! We need to get to them as quickly as possible. People need us to share the truth of God's Word with them so they can be set free.

But despite the great need we see all around us, we must still take the necessary time to prepare. In order to be effective in the ministry, we must first receive what *we* need. Then we'll be equipped to help give people what *they* need.

It's not enough for you to recognize God's call on your life to the ministry. You must also fully prepare so you possess the means to fulfill that call.

It's important for you to develop your *message*, the *spiritual maturity*, and the *practical knowledge* necessary to be successful in the ministry. Your success depends on your diligence to finish your preparation so you can enter the ministry in God's perfect timing.

be teachable

Another requirement for your success in the ministry is that you are *teachable*. If you want to preach and teach the Word effectively to others, you must be teachable yourself.

To be teachable means you're willing to learn more than you already know. It also means being willing to admit when you're wrong.

Did you know it's possible to attend Bible school and take mountains of notes and still be unteachable? Unless you are willing to come in line with the Word that's being taught, you're unteachable.

There is an old saying, "Don't change horses in the middle of the stream." However, spiritually speaking, you can look at that statement in a little different light. If the horse you're riding wants to cross the wrong stream or has fallen dead in the water, you'd *better* change horses!

In other words, if your believing, preaching, or living doesn't line up with the Word, you're going to get yourself in trouble if you aren't willing to change and stay teachable.

Jesus doesn't call *teachers*; He calls those who are *teachable*. You'll always be a student, no matter how experienced you become in the ministry. There will always be new things to learn in the Word and from ministers more experienced than you are. That's why it's so important to always maintain a teachable attitude toward others, as well as toward the Lord.

Even in the natural realm, it's easy to see the value of a teachable attitude. For instance, if you want to learn how to fish, find someone who really understands the art of fishing and make it a point to learn what he knows.

In the church where I served as an associate pastor, there was a man who really knew how to catch fish. Every time he went fishing, he caught his limit.

I once went fishing with this man. I stood within five feet of him. The whole time we were fishing, it seemed like he pulled fish out of the water just as fast as he could get his hook into the water! But I didn't even get one bite!

I never had the desire to become a great fisherman. But if that had been my goal, I would have benefited greatly from taking the time to learn the art of fishing from this man.

On the other hand, I could have been hardheaded and unteachable and said, "I can catch just as many fish as you can! I don't need to listen to you!" But if I'd done that, I sure wouldn't have learned how to fish!

The same principle is true in the ministry. When you're unteachable, you hinder yourself from learning what you need to know to succeed. But staying teachable in every area of the ministry will help you become the best you can be in fulfilling the call of God on your life.

You see, a lot of people go out and fish, but not everyone knows how *to catch* fish. And in the ministry, a lot of people preach, but not everyone knows how to be a fisher of men by ministering in the power of the Holy Spirit!

You can learn many valuable lessons from experienced ministers who are established in the Word and well-acquainted with the Holy Ghost. If you want to walk closely with God and learn to minister in His power, be teachable and open to instruction. For the rest of your life and ministry, make every day an opportunity to learn something valuable in God.

That's how I live my life. I try to learn something new each day, whether it's in the natural or in the spiritual realm. When I get out of bed each morning, I say, "This is the day the Lord has made! I'm going to rejoice and be glad in it, and I expect to learn something new and valuable before I go to sleep tonight."

maintain your personal devotions

Another requirement for success in the ministry is *consistently maintaining times of personal Bible study and daily devotions with the Lord.*

Sometimes when people are preparing for the ministry, the devil tells them, "You hear the Word preached in class all the time. You don't need to take time to read the Bible on your own."

Satan tries the same trick on preachers in active ministry. He tries to make them think that studying the Word for their sermons is enough to keep them spiritually fit and healthy.

But that's a lie! If you neglect your own personal Bible study, you could end up as another statistic on the list of failures in the ministry.

You see, studying the Word for the purpose of teaching it to others has a different effect and impact on your life than studying it for your own edification. Personal study of the Word is what builds your own faith so you can stand against temptations, tests, and trials. Personal Bible study also helps you see yourself as you really are and shows you how to change so you can conform more to the image of Jesus.

It's important for you to understand what I'm saying here, because when you're preparing for ministry there will be times when it will be tempting to neglect your personal devotions. For instance, after you attend Bible school classes, work long hours, and take care of your family, it's easy to think, *We talked about the Bible in class this morning. That's enough Word for today.*

But that's *not* enough! You can't stay strong spiritually if you neglect your own *personal* Bible study. Every day for the rest of your life you'll need the faith-building truth of the Word ministering to your spirit as you study it for yourself. So if you want to succeed in the ministry, don't let anyone or anything keep you from maintaining your own personal daily devotions.

live a life of prayer

Another requirement for success in the ministry is *understanding the importance of prayer.* The simplest definition of prayer is *communing with God.* What breathing is to physical life, praying is to spiritual life. To sustain your physical life, you must breathe air. To maintain a strong spiritual walk, you must live a life of prayer. A strong prayer life is absolutely essential to succeeding in life and in the ministry.

If the only way you can maintain daily prayer time is to get up earlier in the morning, you'd better do it! When I attended Bible school, I knew students who became so busy with activities that they neglected their prayer life. Many of those people never finished Bible school because their relationship with God wasn't first in their lives.

In order to develop an intimate relationship with your Heavenly Father, you need to commune with Him—not just every day, but all day long. David understood the importance of that kind of communion with God. In Psalm 55:17, he said, *"EVENING and MORNING and at NOON I WILL PRAY, and cry aloud, And He shall hear my voice."*

You must learn to come into the Presence of your Heavenly Father and talk to Him as a child would talk to his earthly father. A child doesn't approach his earthly father, afraid and nervous, and say in a stilted, formal voice, "O Father, wilt thou take heed to what I desire?"

No, a child comes to his father and just says, "Daddy, I want to talk to you about something." That's the kind of intimate relationship you should cultivate with God.

When I attended Bible college, some of the students who lived in the dorm with me sometimes said to me, "Hagin, you pray funny."

I'd asked, "What do you mean?"

They'd answer, "Well, you talk to God just like you'd talk to anyone else."

I responded, "That's the way we're supposed to talk to God. He's our Father, and we're His children."

For some reason, many people have the idea that prayer has to be formal to be effective. But we don't have to put on a formal front in order to communicate with God because He's our Father.

When you talk to a friend, you don't speak in a different voice than you normally do, and you don't try to use big, impressive words. You just talk to a friend in a normal voice, as you share what's on your heart. Then you listen to what he has to say. You don't just do all the talking!

That's the way you should communicate with God too! But sometimes people do all the talking and they never listen to what their Heavenly Father has to say!

As you spend time every day communing with your Heavenly Father, you'll learn to hear His voice in your spirit. Your prayer life will become a two-sided conversation. You'll talk to God, and He'll talk to you. And He'll give you comfort, guidance, wisdom—*whatever* you need at the moment.

live a consecrated life

As you prepare to enter the ministry, *living a consecrated Christian life* is a necessity, not a luxury. All your Bible study and praying won't profit you if you don't live consecrated before the Lord, because you can't persist in sin and succeed in the ministry.

I'm not talking about mistakes you've made in the past. If you've asked God's forgiveness for past mistakes, you need to forget them and go on with Him.

However, if there are areas in your life that you haven't consecrated to the Lord, you need to make some adjustments. Ask God to forgive you and allow the blood of Jesus to cleanse you from all unrighteousness (1 John 1:9). Then heed the words of Jesus when He told the woman who had been caught in the act of adultery, *". . . Neither do I condemn you; GO AND SIN NO MORE"* (John 8:11).

Some people ask God's forgiveness and then go out and do the same thing over and over again. They think, *Well, if I sin, afterwards I can just ask God to forgive me, and everything will be all right. I don't really have to change.*

But when a person deliberately persists in willful sin, he's on dangerous ground! The Bible talks about Christians who do that. It says that eventually God has to judge them if they don't judge themselves, repent, and turn away from their sin (Heb. 10:26–31).

You see, what you *do*, how you *act*, and where you *go* are vitally important to your success in the ministry. As one called to the ministry of the Lord Jesus Christ, you have an even greater accountability than a layperson to live a consecrated life (James 3:1). People watch Christians to see how they live. That's especially true of ministers.

You can't preach the Word to someone else if you're not living the Word yourself! So don't allow your Christian testimony to be damaged by pursuing questionable pastimes, like going to dance clubs or bars. Live an honorable life before everyone—saint and sinner alike—by walking in love and integrity toward others.

Living a holy, consecrated life is much easier when you fellowship regularly with other consecrated believers. That's just common sense. So if you want to become a strong Christian, go where committed Christians gather together! You won't be able to keep company with sinners who congregate in worldly places and still stay consecrated in your spiritual walk before the Lord.

The Bible says you are a living epistle, read by all men (2 Cor. 3:2–3). You're the only Bible some people are ever going to read. So determine to live a holy, consecrated life before God.

Ask yourself this question: How many people are influenced for God by watching the way I live? Then make any necessary adjustments so your life will shine as a testimony of the Lord's glory to everyone you meet.

be faithful to your commitment

Another requirement for success in the ministry is *being faithful and committed to your call.*

Faithfulness to your call to the ministry means willingness to do any task the Lord sets before you, regardless of how small it seems. You see, until God can depend upon you in the small things, He can't give you any greater responsibility. For example, God can't make you a pastor of a church or put you behind the pulpit to preach to thousands if you're unfaithful with the small tasks He's given you to do.

The Lord wants to know He can trust you to be faithful in the small tasks, whether it's working in the parking lot, passing the offering bucket, or greeting people at the door.

Some may say, "But I'm called to have a big ministry!" Maybe you are, but do you know where a big ministry begins? It begins in faithfully doing what your hand finds to do as you prepare for the ministry.

Your commitment and determination to be faithful to God's call on your life will hold you steady when hard times come and it seems like fulfilling your ministry is an unreachable goal.

Success in the ministry comes when you learn to be faithful and committed, even when it hurts your flesh. For instance, you must be willing to go where the Lord wants you to go, even when you don't want to go there. If you're called to preach, you'll have to be committed to preach the Word, even when you don't feel like it.

I know what it's like to preach when your flesh is hurting and you don't feel like preaching. I remember one time the RHEMA Singers and Band traveled with me to hold some meetings at a particular church. One afternoon before the evening service, we were all playing basketball in the church gym, and I injured my ankle.

Some of the band members said, "You can't even walk! What are you going to do about preaching tonight?"

I answered, "I'm just going to get up there and preach!"

One of the band members said, "But you can't even get a shoe on that foot!"

"Who is advertised to preach at the meeting tonight?" I asked.

"You are."

"That's right. And I'll be there to preach!" I said. "I have to be faithful to fulfill what I'm called to do."

Although I was believing for my ankle to be healed, when it came time for the evening service, the healing hadn't manifested yet. Somehow I managed to stuff my swollen foot into my shoe, with my ankle still hurting like fire!

But once I stepped onto the platform and began preaching, the anointing of God came on me. I walked up and down that platform as I preached, and my ankle didn't hurt at all! Because I was faithful and committed to my call to preach, the power of God supernaturally enabled me to minister to those people that night.

You see, even in the ministry, you don't always feel like doing everything you have to do. And as you prepare for the ministry, there will probably be some days you'd rather not get out of bed and face your daily responsibilities. Even when you're in the full-time ministry, there will probably be times you wish you could retreat to a cabin in the wilderness, far away from people and their problems.

Those are the times when you'll need to reach down into your spirit past your initial excitement about your call, and draw upon your deep commitment *to fulfill* that call. Faithfulness to that commitment will hold you steady, no matter what you might *feel* at the moment.

As you trust and rely upon God's ability inside you, He'll enable you to overcome every temptation to get discouraged in the hard times. Just determine *never* to give up, and keep on serving the Lord. Then God will count you faithful to His call on your life.

learn to give freely into **GOD**'s kingdom

Another requirement for success in the ministry is *learning to give freely out of your substance.*

When some people think about giving, they think only about giving *money*. That's an important part of giving, but we can also give our *talents* and our *time* to the work of God's Kingdom. Actually, to be successful in the ministry, you must willingly give everything you are and everything you possess to the Lord to use as He wills.

When it comes to giving finances, some people who live on a tight budget make excuses to explain why they don't tithe or give offerings. For instance, they say, "I just don't make enough money to pay tithes." But if a person willingly brings his tithe into the storehouse, he'll begin to see how far God will stretch the other nine-tenths of his income!

In the early years of my ministry when our income was very limited, my wife told me, "Honey, this month we have more money going out to pay bills than we have coming in." But despite what our financial situation looked like in the natural, we faithfully paid our tithes first before we paid any of our other bills.

At the end of that month, we found that after giving to God and paying every bill, we still had five dollars left over! To this day, we don't know where the extra money came from.

But, you see, if you're faithful to God, He'll be faithful to you. If you give of your time, talents, and money to the work of His Kingdom, He'll give back abundantly to you.

I read a story once about a five-year-old girl who came home from kindergarten one day and told her parents, "Each of us in our class is going to bring one of our toys to give to poor children. The girls are supposed to bring one of their dolls."

So this little girl lined up all of her dolls and pondered which one she wanted to give to a poor little girl. Finally she decided to give away her favorite doll. Then she dressed the doll that she loved so much in the best dress she could find and fixed it up so it would look pretty.

The little girl clutched her doll as she ate dinner that evening, and she took it to bed with her that night. The next morning before school, she held that favorite doll tightly, crying at the thought of saying good-bye to it.

The little girl's daddy said to her, "You know, Honey, you don't have to give away your *best* doll."

But the little girl wiped away her tears and said, "Yes, I do, Daddy. I wouldn't give a bad doll to anyone." With that, she cheered up and skipped down the road to school.

That Christmas, this little girl received a special gift. It was the very best doll money could buy. As the little girl looked with wide eyes at her beautiful new doll, she exclaimed, "I guess when you give God *your* best, He gives you *His* best!"

That little girl was right! If you give God your best, He will bless your life and ministry far beyond what you could ever imagine!

These are some vital requirements I have learned for success in the ministry. It's important to understand that these requirements ensure your success, not only in your preparation time, but also as you do the work God has called you to.

So be diligent and teachable as you prepare to enter the ministry. For the rest of your life, make it your highest priority to spend time every day in personal Bible study and communion with God.

Live a consecrated life, staying faithful and committed to your call, no matter what circumstances you may face. Finally, give your very best to the Lord, expecting Him to bless you abundantly with all you need to accomplish the task He's given you. When you make that kind of commitment and dedication, you're setting yourself on a course that leads to success in God!

chapter seven

endure hardness
as a good soldier

he Apostle Paul advised Timothy, a younger minister in age and experience, to ". . . *endure hardness*, as a good soldier of Jesus Christ" (2 Tim. 2:3 *KJV*).
That's good counsel for anyone who is called to be a soldier
in the ministry of Jesus Christ.

The truth is, overcoming all the obstacles to entering
the ministry isn't easy. I'm not trying to be negative. I'm just
stating a fact. The Bible says that people are destroyed for
lack of knowledge (Hosea 4:6). Many people who are called
of God fall by the wayside before the Lord can ever use
them, because no one told them the truth about the pressures they'd have to face and overcome in the ministry.

make up your mind you'll *never* quit

I didn't say that just because there are pressures in
ministry, you *won't* succeed. I said it won't always be easy.
Get it clear in your mind once and for all that choosing to
walk by faith in God's Word doesn't mean you'll never experience opposition or trials.

Some people preach that walking by faith means never
having any problems. But they didn't find that doctrine in

the Bible. Even Jesus said, "*. . . In the world you WILL have tribulation; but be of good cheer, I have overcome the world*" (John 16:33).

That's why you should make up your mind before you ever enter the ministry that you are going to hold fast to your commitment to God's call, no matter what circumstances may come your way.

Make the quality decision, "It makes no difference what the devil tries to throw in my path. I *will* endure hardness as a good soldier of Jesus Christ. I will successfully complete my ministerial training and go on to fulfill my call to the ministry!"

When I joined the Army and was on my way to boot camp, I made that kind of decision. I told myself, *I won't allow any hardship or any drill sergeant in this army to keep me from becoming a successful soldier!*

Many times in boot camp, that decision helped me overcome difficult challenges. Basic training wasn't easy, but I never did join the other soldiers when they complained about the hardships. Boot camp wasn't the ordeal to me that it was to some of the other soldiers because I had already set my mind on succeeding.

You need to make the same kind of decision in ministry. Your decision to never give up will hold you steady when you encounter pressures and problems. As you move on with God, the enemy will try to detour you from fully completing the call. When he does, remind yourself of *the day and hour* when you made the quality decision that *nothing* would keep you from fulfilling God's call.

You'll also need to remind the devil in no uncertain terms of that decision. Tell him, "Mr. Devil, I proclaimed in

Jesus' Name that you and your demons aren't big enough, strong enough, or mean enough to stop me from fulfilling my ministry. I *won't* be deterred from finishing my course. With God's Word, I'll overcome every obstacle, every problem, and every trial!"

Let me give you an example of the kind of hardness, or hardship, a person may have to endure as he prepares for the ministry. A person will probably feel pressure if he goes to Bible school and has very little money to live on.

He'll feel even more pressure if he has to work a full shift at a job in the evening or at night while going to classes during the day, writing school papers, and studying textbooks. If he is married, he also has the needs of his family to consider.

On top of all *those* pressures, add the *devil's* strategies against him. For instance, in the midst of everything else, what will he do if his car unexpectedly breaks down?

The devil uses problems like that to try to cause a person to explode and yell at his roommate, his boss, his wife, his children, and everyone around him! Then the enemy wants him to throw up his hands in despair and condemnation and just quit, never to fulfill his call to the ministry.

Unfortunately, sometimes that's exactly what happens to people who haven't made the quality decision never to give up in the ministry, regardless of the pressures they will face. They haven't learned how to endure a few hardships as good soldiers of Jesus Christ.

I had to decide to endure hardship when I joined the military. And my determination to never quit made it a lot easier for me to finish basic training. Other soldiers who didn't have that kind of determination gave up in the middle of training and had to "recycle." That means they had to start basic training all over again.

So as you prepare for the ministry, make the decision to endure hardness as a good soldier of Jesus Christ. If you don't, when the devil puts pressure on you, you may get thrown off course and have to "recycle" in your training.

In other words, you may have to back up and do your first works again (Rev. 2:5). You'll have to become established in the Word and in your fellowship with the Lord all over again before the Lord can release you to go into active ministry.

be strong in the Lord

However, don't ever try to endure hardness in your own strength. Your key to success in the ministry is to be strong *in the Lord*, not in yourself (Eph. 6:10).

2 TIMOTHY 2:1
1 You therefore, my son, BE STRONG IN THE GRACE THAT IS IN CHRIST JESUS.

Paul wrote these words to Timothy when Paul was facing death. He was about to be executed by the Romans on the false charge that he was a revolutionary against the state.

Timothy was Paul's spiritual son and disciple (1 Tim. 1:18). Timothy helped Paul in the spiritual oversight of some of the churches that were scattered throughout Asia. Paul knew that once he died, Timothy would be responsible to help continue spreading the Gospel.

As Timothy's spiritual father, Paul was concerned about how well Timothy would do once he was on his own.

Could Timothy stand up under the pressure of his minis-terial responsibilities? Could he handle the problems he'd face and the difficult circumstances that might arise? Would he continue to diligently study the Word, pray, and preach the Word?

We can tell by reading Paul's admonitions to Timothy that these were questions and concerns on Paul's heart. Paul knew Timothy had only one hope to be successful in the ministry, just as any of us called to the ministry have only one hope. The *only* way Timothy could successfully overcome in times of pressure and hardship was by standing strong *in the grace that's in Christ Jesus.*

In our human strength we're no match for the devil's strategies and the pressures that inevitably arise in the ministry. And we'll end up lying in the dust of our own weaknesses if we attempt to overcome problems and fulfill our ministry according to our own abilities.

Actually, a person fails when he tries to accomplish *anything* for God in his own strength. No matter who the person is or what he thinks he can do, his endeavors will eventually end in failure if he doesn't know how to be strong in the Lord.

But God's strength is entirely different from our puny human strength. God's strength is all-sufficient and all-powerful. And as we stand fast in our faith in God's Word, His power *can* and *will* conquer every obstacle we encounter.

So no matter how well-known you may become in the ministry or how long your list of accomplishments, never forget that you are nothing except in Christ and in *His* strength. I don't care how great you can preach or how well you can do *anything* in the ministry, you aren't going to accomplish anything *for God* without the power of the Holy Spirit.

Never forget to stand strong in the matchless grace of the Son of God. Remind yourself occasionally that the things you accomplish in your life are only a result of God strengthening you and giving you the knowledge and supernatural ability to fulfill His will.

If you start receiving glory for yourself, you'll fail in the ministry. Without the strength of Jesus Christ to empower and equip you, your accomplishments in the ministry will amount to exactly *nothing!*

God alone deserves the glory and honor for anything you or I achieve in the ministry. We can't stick our thumbs under our lapels and say, "Look what *my* faith accomplished!"

Actually, you could make faith confessions all day in your own strength, and nothing would happen. Certainly you play a part in God's promises coming to pass by believing God's Word and exercising your faith. But it's *God's* power and strength that causes the answer to come. So God gets all the credit—*not* you!

Therefore, the secret to your success in the ministry is to learn how to tap into the grace and strength of God. With *His* strength, you can achieve any task God asks you to do for Him. His strength will carry you through every crisis of life. Sometimes every circumstance in the natural will scream at you, "You aren't going to make it this time!" But God's power and grace will see you through to victory.

When you stand strong in the Lord, you'll be able to look the enemy in the face and say, "Oh, no, Mr. Devil! You can't trespass on my property! I come against you, not in my strength or in my name, but in the powerful Name of the Lord Jesus Christ, my Savior, Baptizer, Healer, and soon-coming King. In the Name of Jesus, I come against you, not because of *who* I am, but because of *Whose* I am. And although I can't do anything of myself, I can do *all* things through Christ Who strengthens me!"

overcoming the devil's pressures

There are some pressures in the ministry that every minister faces because he isn't perfect himself, and because he has to deal with imperfect people who have needs and problems. That's what life and ministry are all about. However, normal pressures of life are nothing to be alarmed about. A person just needs to learn to continually cast all his cares on the Lord and rely on God's strength and wisdom to handle each situation correctly.

But besides these normal pressures of the ministry, there are also the additional pressures the devil uses to try to get you out of the will of God. A dictionary definition of *pressure* is "a pressing, compressing, or squeezing." The devil tries to cause difficult circumstances and problems to arise to make you feel pressured, squeezed, or burdened in life.

Paul certainly knew what that felt like. For instance, when talking about his ministry in Asia, he said, ". . . *WE WERE BURDENED BEYOND MEASURE, above strength, so that we despaired even of life*" (2 Cor. 1:8).

Satan knows that if he can pressure you and burden you and squeeze you out of God's will, then he's won a victory and God has lost a good soldier. That's why you have to use your authority in Christ to stand against the enemy's pressures so he doesn't gain a foothold in your life.

You see, those who are called to the ministry are destined to be a major force for God in the revival of these last days. The devil knows that, and that's why he has made Christians who minister one of his major targets. He's going to do everything in his power to stop that mighty force—*you*—from going forth full of the Holy Ghost and equipped with the Word of God.

So keep standing strong in the Lord as you answer your call. Endure hardness as a good soldier of Jesus Christ, for the devil will try to hinder you by putting obstacles in your path.

Satan will do his best to deter and discourage you. He wants to turn you aside from what God has called you to do before you ever get started. He knows that the more you are trained in God's Word and in your authority in Christ, the less opportunity he will have to defeat you down the road.

examples of satan's pressures

One of the first ways Satan tries to pressure people so they are hindered from answering their call is in the area of finances. When he starts putting pressure on people's finances, some believers want to bolt and run. Others just wring their hands and moan, "What are we going to do now?" Still others act foolishly in presumption. For example, they may write a check when they know there's no money in the bank, all the while claiming they're in faith. But those aren't scriptural ways to respond to Satan's pressures.

In the early years of my ministry, my wife, Lynette, set a good example by the way she responded to financial pressures. In 1965, I had recently been discharged from the Army, and my wife and I were newly married. My wife worked a secular job and I was looking for opportunities to preach. However, things weren't going the way I had expected. I wasn't finding many open doors to preach.

Then I received an offer of a good position with the U.S. State Department. The government was interested in my qualifications because I had worked in communications in the Army.

Although I knew I was called to the ministry, I was tempted to accept the government position. As a husband, it was upsetting to think that I wasn't able to adequately provide for my new wife. And of course, the enemy uses times like this to open doors of opportunity to cause you to get out of the will of God.

I am very grateful my wife was so supportive during this difficult time. She encouraged me and never gave up on me or my call to the ministry. So even though we knew we would endure some financial hardships, we agreed I would not take that job and we would stay in the ministry.

Thank God for good wives! I can say that, to a large extent, I'm where I am today in the ministry because I have a good wife who was willing to sacrifice with me as we got started in the ministry.

For several years, we didn't have much financially. When my son, Craig, was born in 1969, we lived in a tiny house that was poorly insulated. In the winter, the cold north wind howled through the cracks in the old window frames.

We owned an old car with engine problems, but we didn't have the money to get it fixed. In the wintertime, we'd have to push that car to get it started.

But my wife was a minister's daughter, and she understood the pressures that sometimes come in the ministry. She said, "It's all right that we have to make sacrifices now.

As we continue to obey God, we'll eventually come out on top." And she was right! God has supplied all of our needs, more abundantly than we could ever have imagined.

No, getting started in the ministry isn't always easy. Most of the time you won't start off preaching to thousands or receiving large offerings. You'll probably have to endure some hardships.

Will you hold fast to your call to the ministry even in the midst of financial pressure? You see, it's easy to shout, "My God is bigger than any problem!" when you're not facing any major problems. But what will you do if you find yourself in a situation where the rent and the car payment are overdue, the kitchen cupboards are bare, and you don't have any money in the bank?

What are you going to do when you feel as though there's nowhere to turn for help, and the devil is bombarding you with thoughts such as, *You were stupid to leave the security of that job so you could prepare for the ministry!*

That's when you find out if you really believe that God is bigger than any problem! That's the time to trust in the Lord with all your heart and call upon His supernatural power to work on your behalf.

God's power *will* work for you when you claim His promises by faith (Phil. 4:19). But the situation may not turn around overnight. You may have to stand in faith on God's Word without wavering for a while before you see your answer manifested. However, I promise you this—you stay faithful to God, and He *will* abundantly reward you.

Satan may also try to put pressure on you through other people who are close to you. For instance, sometimes a person feels pressured because his relatives are against him answering his call to the ministry. They may not understand why he would leave a good-paying job to go to Bible school. It may not make any sense to them at all!

What do you do when you encounter that kind of pressure? The Bible says, *"MANY are the AFFLICTIONS of the righteous, But THE LORD DELIVERS HIM OUT OF THEM ALL"* (Ps. 34:19).

That word *afflictions* can also be translated "tests and trials." Well, it's a test and a trial if your relatives and friends come against you for answering your call to the ministry. Opposition from loved ones is painful when all you want to do is obey God.

But a strong soldier of Jesus Christ endures hardship! He lets the oil of the Holy Spirit heal any wounds that people might inflict on him. Then he comes out on the other side of every trial victoriously because he trusts in God to deliver him, and he refuses to quit.

what to do when satan pressures you

How you handle the devil's pressures largely determines the outcome of your life and ministry. Unless you learn how to respond scripturally to the enemy's pressures, it will be easy to quit when the going gets tough.

How should you respond scripturally when the devil puts pressure on you? The first thing you need to do is *reconfirm in your heart that you are truly called of God to the ministry.* Go back in your mind to the time you first realized God was calling you to do something for Him. Let those memories serve as an anchor to hold you fast when the devil sends the winds of trial and adversity against you and tries to blow you off course.

After you've reconfirmed in your heart that you're called to the ministry, the second thing you need to do when the enemy puts pressure on you is *determine God's specific instructions on HOW to fulfill that call.*

For instance, I could call to someone across the room, "Hey, I'd like you to help me do something." If that person answers, "Okay," and walks over to help me, that means he is *willing* to help me. But he won't know *how* to help me until I tell him what I want him to do.

You may have accepted the call of God on your life, but now you need to understand *how* God wants you to fulfill that call. It's very important to follow the Holy Spirit's leading as you answer your call. You make it much more difficult for Satan to sidetrack you with his pressures when you know you're in the *center* of God's will.

But once you've sought the Lord and determined you're doing what He wants you to do, don't fool yourself by thinking you'll never encounter pressure and obstacles from the enemy. It's important to realize that you're not going to be able to avoid Satan's pressures altogether just because you're in God's will. Satan is the god of this world (2 Cor. 4:4 *KJV*), and as long as you're living on this earth, you'll have to deal with the enemy and resist his strategies in the Name of Jesus.

Look in the New Testament at the ministries of Peter and Paul. They both knew they were called of God to preach the Gospel. They both knew their specific assignments from the Lord. But even though they were fulfilling the will of

God, Peter and Paul still faced major opposition and obstacles in the ministry.

For instance, Paul knew that God had called him to preach to the Gentiles. Paul's ministry required him to travel, preaching and teaching in various places. But wherever he went, he had to deal with hostile Jews who opposed the gospel message and tried to hinder and harm him (Acts 13:45,50; 14:19).

So Satan *will* try to pressure you even when you're doing God's will. However, be sure you're not encountering unnecessary pressures and problems because you're *out* of God's will. If you find out you've taken a detour, don't just stay in the situation and suffer that unnecessary pressure. Seek the Lord and find out how to get back in His will!

Some people say, "Well, I hate to admit I made a mistake." But it's better to admit you've made a mistake than to compound your problems by staying out of God's will!

Also, don't be too quick to say, "The Lord told me . . ." to try to prove that you're in God's will unless you're really sure you heard from God. Some people are always trying to add credibility to what they're doing by saying, "The Lord told me to do this."

But you don't have to try to convince people you've heard from God. If you've really heard from God, and you obey His direction, people will know by the results that it was God leading and guiding you.

When you know you're obeying God, you can be assured that your steps are being ordered by the Lord (Ps. 37:23). There is such peace in knowing that the mighty God Who stood on the edge of space and spoke the worlds into existence and placed each heavenly body into its orbit is the same Almighty God Who now leads and guides you!

If God is big enough to create and uphold the universe by the word of His power (Heb. 1:3), He is certainly big enough to deliver you from every one of the enemy's tactics and guide you into His perfect will for your life!

The third thing you need to do when Satan puts pressure on you is *maintain a confident attitude of faith.* Your attitude in the midst of the pressures of ministry has everything to do with your success.

No one, including ministers, is exempt from tests, trials, and problems. We've all had our share. But whether or not we come through those trials victoriously depends on how we choose to believe, think, and respond in the midst of them.

So stand fast in faith on the Word of God and say, "Mr. Devil, my God's grace is sufficient. And He said that He *would* deliver me out of every single trial you would try to throw at me (2 Tim. 3:11). Devil, you can't drive me out of the ministry. I *am* going to do what God has told me to do!" Holding steady in faith with that kind of determination is enduring hardness as a good soldier!

Maintaining a confident attitude of faith is crucial, because sometimes the ministry can seem like a pressure cooker. Do you know how a pressure cooker works? The lid is tightly sealed so the pressure will build up when the heat is increased. The pressure causes the food in the pot to cook quickly.

To keep the pot from building up too much pressure and exploding, the lid has a release valve so steam can escape. As the pressure builds up in the pot, the release valve lets off steam.

When you are feeling as though your life is a pressure cooker ready to explode, remember to relieve the pressure with the release valve God has provided for you. Your release valve is your faith in the anointed Word of God.

The devil will try to plug up your release valve by causing your mind to be consumed with the cares of this world. Then he'll turn up the heat by bringing problems and trials your way. He wants the pressure to build up in your life until you're in despair, crying, "I don't know what I'm going to do. It looks like I'm going to fail!"

But you can keep the devil from succeeding in his evil strategies against you. Don't let him plug up your safety valve! Keep quoting the Word to him. Tell him, "Devil, you won't defeat me! I can do all things through Christ Who strengthens me! In Him I am more than a conqueror!" (Phil. 4:13; Rom. 8:37).

As you steadfastly confess the promises of God's Word in faith, you'll watch as the pressures the devil is trying to bring against you begin to dissipate and disappear. Natural circumstances may still look difficult for a while, but your faith in God's Word will bring you release from oppression and pressure.

And as you keep your mind focused on the Word instead of on the problems, the Holy Spirit within will strengthen you so you can come through those tests and trials victoriously!

The fourth thing you should do when Satan's pressures come your way is *praise God in the midst of the trial.* I've made that a practice in my own life. When I encounter a problem, I immediately begin praising the Lord for the answer.

I say, "Father, I thank and praise You, because in Christ Jesus I always triumph! I praise You for Your faithfulness to Your Word. No problem is too big for You, Lord. Thank You for causing me to be victorious, no matter what tries to come against me!"

Concentrating on praising the Lord always changes my mental outlook. Instead of getting upset about the problem, I can rest in my faith in God's ability to bring a *solution* to the problem.

Praising God from your heart will always change your mental attitude and bring victory where defeat once seemed to loom on the horizon. For instance, you could choose to sit alone in your home and feel depressed. You could fill your mind with thoughts such as, *How can I do everything I need to do? I have so much to do to get ready for the ministry, not to mention all my other personal responsibilities. It's just too much!*

But the more you think negatively, the worse you'll feel. Soon you'll feel completely overwhelmed, and Satan will succeed in discouraging you.

In that kind of situation, just begin praising God for Who He is and what He has promised to do for you in His Word. As you focus on the goodness and the faithfulness of God, you'll find your attitude will begin to change.

The mental oppression will leave, and you'll begin to experience God's peace that surpasses all understanding (Phil. 4:6–7). Then you'll be in a position to receive God's wisdom and strength so you can fight the good fight of faith and overcome Satan's strategies in your life.

fight the good fight of faith

As long as I can remember, my dad taught me through his own example how to endure hardness as a good soldier of Jesus Christ. Through his example, I learned how to fight the good fight of faith.

I remember times when I was growing up that things were tough financially. Sometimes we didn't even have food in our kitchen cupboards. But never once did I see my father tell anyone that we were in need. He always trusted the Lord to meet our needs, and God always came through for us.

Never once did I hear my dad tell God, "Lord, I'm doing Your will and You aren't blessing me" or "Oh, Lord, bless me." When we were in the midst of the most difficult situations, Dad would take authority over the devil's strategies against him.

But all I ever heard Dad say to the Lord was, "Oh, Lord, for those who are lost and dying, and for those who are suffering with sickness as I once suffered—send someone to tell them about Jesus. And, Lord, make *me* a blessing to others."

Dad never quit fighting the good fight of faith, regardless of the hardships he sometimes faced. That's the kind of tenacity you need to cultivate in your faith walk. When the enemy tries to put pressure on you, rebuke him. Look him square in the face and say, "Devil, I've just begun to fight!"

Those were like the words spoken by the great American naval officer John Paul Jones as he faced what seemed to be certain defeat during the Revolutionary War.

John Paul Jones spoke those words during a major sea battle with the British as he stood on the deck of his battered ship. British cannonballs had tattered the sails of his ship and destroyed the mainmast. Jones' ship looked like it was going to sink at any minute. Thinking his victory was assured, the British commander sent Jones the message, "Are you ready to give up?"

But John Paul Jones hoisted his battle flag high and sent back the courageous reply, "I have not yet begun to fight!" Despite the damage inflicted on his own ship, Jones went on to capture the British flagship and win the battle.

Friend, when the devil tries to buffet your ship on the sea of life until it looks as though it's about to sink, you have to take a courageous stand on the Word of God. Satan is going to ask you, "Are you ready to give up?" But instead of giving up, raise your victory flag high and tell him, "Mr. Devil, you can't defeat me! I have not yet begun to fight!"

I'm talking about fighting the good fight of faith. That's the only fight God has called you to fight. You can never take a vacation from that fight, because the devil never does. There will never be an opportunity to sit back and let your guard down. Satan is always prowling about, looking for someone to devour (1 Peter 5:8). That's why you must learn to endure hardness as a good soldier of Jesus Christ and stand your ground.

The Lord once said something to me about the good fight of faith. He said, "If you learn how to follow Me, troubles and afflictions in the ministry will only mean greater victories."

Then He took me through the Bible, showing me how that principle is demonstrated through the lives of many in the Bible. From Moses in the Book of Exodus to the Apostle John on the Isle of Patmos where he penned the Book of Revelation, I saw that people who experienced the greatest trials often experienced the greatest victories.

For instance, look at what happened to the prophet Daniel. From his youth, Daniel lived a blameless, godly life, even as a captive in the courts of the Babylonian kings. But the day came when evil men who were jealous of Daniel devised a scheme to get him thrown into a lions' den (Dan. 6:4–13).

Things looked bad for Daniel when they threw him into that lions' den. The lions were roaring with hunger, and he was their meal! But Daniel knew the power of his God, and he trusted God to deliver him. So Daniel probably just laid down, used a lion for a pillow, and got a peaceful night's sleep!

When the soldiers opened the pit the next morning, King Darius cried, *". . . Daniel, servant of the living God, has your God, whom you serve continually, been able to deliver you from the lions?"* (Dan. 6:20).

Daniel calmly responded, *". . . O king, live forever! My God sent His angel and shut the lions' mouths, so that they have not hurt me . . ."* (Dan. 6:21–22).

It certainly was a trial to be thrown into a lions' den! But because Daniel knew his God and trusted in His goodness and power to deliver him, that trial led to a great victory for Daniel. Not only was Daniel's life miraculously spared, but Darius issued a decree, commanding people throughout the land to acknowledge Daniel's God as the true and living God (Dan. 6:25–27).

In the ministry, sooner or later, you will face your own "lions' den"—circumstances that look impossible to overcome. The devil will try to make you succumb to fear, because fear opens the door to defeat.

But when you're in the lions' den, start quoting the promises in God's Word at the devil and at the adverse circumstances. Take your stand on God's Word in faith and refuse to budge. Then go to sleep, using the problem for a pillow! In other words, enter the rest of faith and allow God to turn around the problem for your good.

You may have to sleep in the lions' den for a little while. But in the end, you'll walk out free—*if* you don't give up fighting the good fight of faith with God's Word.

count it all joy

Understanding that tests and trials can be your stepping-stones to greater victories will make it easier to obey the biblical admonition: *"My brethren, COUNT IT ALL JOY when you fall into various trials"* (James 1:2).

I'll give you another reason you can count it all joy when you encounter tests and trials. Greater opposition from the enemy often means that the devil isn't happy with what you're doing for God.

You see, if you were following your own plans and refusing to answer your call, the devil wouldn't need to oppose you so much. But when you obey God's call, you threaten the devil. He knows only too well the threat you'll be to his kingdom once you're trained in the Word of God and you know how to be led by the Holy Spirit.

So when pressures and problems come your way, rejoice! Realize that your obedience to God has the devil running scared! Satan might try his best to keep you from learning how to be successful in the ministry. But he can't do one thing to you if you stand strong in your authority in Christ and refuse to allow him to gain a foothold in your life.

James gives one more reason you can consider it all joy in the midst of trials. He says, *"knowing that THE TESTING OF YOUR FAITH PRODUCES PATIENCE* (James 1:3). Allow the pressures and problems you encounter to mold and mature you into a person of strong faith.

Don't look at the trouble and the trial. Look to the Victor, Jesus Christ (Heb. 12:2). Don't allow your heart to be troubled in the midst of life's storms. Rest in the Lord, and He will bring peace and calm to your heart and mind.

God called and you responded. The Lord will honor your obedience. He won't ever leave you or forsake you (Heb. 13:5). No matter what you face, if you refuse to give up, you can always call upon God's supernatural power to overcome the devil's opposition.

characteristics of a good soldier

To endure hardness as a good soldier of Jesus Christ, it's important for you to know some characteristics of a good soldier. Here are two of those characteristics.

First, a good soldier *never shirks his responsibility.* He doesn't lag behind or seek to escape the battle. He doesn't hide from the labor and toil of carrying his own load. He knows that if he doesn't fulfill his responsibility on the battlefield, it could endanger the lives of his fellow soldiers.

For instance, in air battles during World War II, bombers flew in formation, and each plane was assigned a particular position. If the pilots didn't stay in their positions, they left a gap in the formation which made the other planes vulnerable to enemy attack and increased the risk of the planes getting shot down.

The same is true in God's army. Each believer has a particular responsibility to fulfill. When one person shirks his responsibility, it can cause spiritual hardship on others, making them more vulnerable to the enemy's attacks. That is particularly true when ministers run from their call and fail to fulfill their responsibilities in the ministry.

On the other hand, the gates of hell cannot prevail against the Body of Christ when believers take their places and stand in their God-given authority as faithful soldiers in God's army!

Second, a good soldier *obeys the commander*. For instance, in boot camp in the Army, we learned to obey orders instantly without hesitating or arguing. Later I talked to soldiers I'd trained with after they returned from Vietnam. They told me that instantly responding to the commanding officer's orders saved their lives many times.

Spiritually speaking, whether or not you receive the blessings of God hinges upon your obedience to Jesus Christ, your Commander-in-Chief. Jesus will reveal His will to you by the Holy Spirit within. Your obedience to Him will help you overcome the devil's strategies so you can walk in the fullness of God's purpose for you. And your ability to instantly obey the leading of the Holy Spirit will keep you from harm or unnecessary hardship.

You must also submit to the people God has placed in authority over you, following them as they follow Christ

(1 Cor. 11:1; Phil. 3:17). A person can never be a real leader until he has learned to be a good follower.

However, good leaders don't have the attitude, *I'm the boss! Therefore, I always have the final say-so!* In the Kingdom of God, the Bible teaches that all believers, leaders and followers alike, are to submit one to another in humility of spirit (Eph. 5:21; 1 Peter 5:5). Jesus is actually the Commander of the Body of Christ, and we're all subject to *Him* and then to each other. That's true biblical submission.

endure hardness by walking in the Spirit

Another factor in enduring hardness as a good soldier of Jesus Christ is to learn how to walk in the Spirit. That means maintaining a vital prayer life with the Lord and staying in the Word.

It also means living a disciplined life of continually putting your flesh under and resisting temptation. Paul said, *". . . I DISCIPLINE MY BODY AND BRING IT INTO SUBJECTION, lest, when I have preached to others, I myself should become disqualified"* (1 Cor. 9:27).

There will be times while preparing for the ministry when your body won't want to get out of bed. Your body will tell you, "You're too tired! You worked late. You deserve a rest from going to class," or "You can't minister to others. You need someone to minister to *you!*" But who are you going to listen to? Your body or your spirit?

When your spirit man reminds you that God promises to quicken your mortal body by the Holy Spirit (Rom. 8:11 *KJV*), you must obey your spirit and say, "All right, Lord, I'm getting out of this bed. But I need the Holy Spirit to quicken my mortal body." When you do that, the Holy Spirit will honor your faith in God's Word. His strength will enable you to do what He's called you to do that day.

be a strong finisher!

You must make a habit of putting your body under subjection to your spirit every day. That will enable you to be a strong finisher in the race God has set before you in the ministry.

Your first goal in running your race in the ministry is to finish your time of preparation. Then when God says you're ready to enter the ministry, you must determine to fulfill your call step by step until the day you can confidently say, "I've finished my course!"

You have a divine mission to accomplish! And *you* are the only one who can decide whether you'll finish or quit in fulfilling that mission.

So refuse to let yourself waste precious energy and time on what your flesh wants to do. Concentrate on finishing strong in your spiritual race so you don't fall by the wayside. Don't drag yourself across the finish line long after others have completed their race and are enjoying the rewards of obedience.

Somewhere in this lost and hurting world, people are waiting for *you* to finish your preparation time so you can enter the ministry. God has ordained that you touch their lives with the love of Jesus.

Those people don't need an ill-prepared, ill-equipped minister of the Gospel who has never learned to withstand Satan's pressures and endure hardship. They need someone who will be faithful when the going gets tough—someone who has paid the price of obedience to become a good soldier of Jesus Christ.

Yes, you'll have to overcome pressures and problems at times. It won't always be easy to hold fast to your calling. But don't let the devil deter you from fulfilling what God has called you to do.

Make the quality decision that you *will* successfully complete your "basic training" in the ministry, no matter what obstacles might stand in your way. Then throughout your life, allow God to continue to prepare you for every purpose He has planned for you. Learn to endure hardship as a good soldier of Jesus Christ, so you can finish strong in your appointed course of ministry!

practical advice to ministers

guarding
your family

i would like to share some practical advice to help you be more effective in the ministry. I learned a lot growing up in a minister's home, and I've learned a great deal more after nearly 50 years of personal experience in the ministry.

One important thing I've learned is that ministers must be careful to *guard their family.* Except for a minister's relationship with the Lord, the minister's family should come before everything else in life—including the ministry he or she is called to fulfill.

God established marriage and the family long before He instituted the Church (Gen. 2:22–25; 4:1–2). The family unit is *very* important to the Lord. He expects you to make your family the highest priority in your life.

Think about it. Yes, you may be called to the ministry. But if you win the whole world and lose your own family, what have you really gained? Your spouse and your children are the most precious possessions God has given you. And He doesn't want you to fulfill *your* call at the expense of *their* welfare.

satan targets the family

The family is one of the devil's main targets in these last days. That's why one of my highest priorities is to help ministers understand how to guard their family from the enemy's strategies.

You must stay sensible and alert to the devil's attempts to find an open door to attack your family. If you're not aware of his schemes and devices, you can become complacent, relax your stance of faith, and end up getting thrown out of the saddle. In other words, you can find yourself thrown off course, out of the will of God.

I found out what it was like to almost get *literally* thrown out of the saddle years ago when I visited my uncle's ranch. I told my uncle I'd help him bring his cattle in from the field so the calves could be vaccinated.

I mounted a horse named Calico Bay that was expertly trained to herd cattle. I rode Calico Bay out to the range to bring in the cows, and at first, everything went fine. The cows obediently moved in the direction I wanted them to go. I sat on the horse, almost half asleep from the monotony of watching hundreds of cows move past me toward the barn.

All of a sudden, one cow decided she didn't want to go to the barn. She bolted and ran away in the opposite direction from the rest of the herd. Without any prompting from me, Calico Bay took off at a gallop to chase that stray cow. That horse was so well trained, she knew exactly what to do.

The only problem was, I'd been sitting relaxed in the saddle, almost falling asleep! I sure wasn't ready for any sudden movement! When Calico Bay turned abruptly to chase that cow, my feet lost their hold in the stirrups. If I hadn't grabbed hold of the saddle horn, I would have been thrown out of the saddle and dumped on the ground!

Since the horse knew exactly what to do to herd that cow back to the rest of the cattle, I gave up trying to guide her with the reins and just hung on for dear life! Once the cow was safely guided back to the herd where it belonged, Calico Bay settled down. Only then was I able to get my feet back into the stirrups and sit up straight in the saddle again.

My experience with that horse paints a good picture of what the devil tries to do to you and your family if you don't keep your guard up. Everything may be going smoothly in your lives. Then all of a sudden, the devil throws a problem into the middle of your plans.

If you're not ready for the devil's attack, and if you don't exercise your authority in Christ over him, you could find yourself desperately trying to hang on to victory with only one hand. You could even end up crashing to the ground in defeat.

make your marriage work

Stay alert so you can guard your family from Satan's attacks. Do everything you can to protect your relationship with your spouse, because your ministry will only be as successful as your marriage.

The devil knows a divided house cannot stand (Mark 3:25), so he'll do everything he can to cause division between a husband and wife. Unfortunately, too many husbands and wives allow Satan to get a foothold in their marriage through strife and selfishness. Never have so many

Christian marriages ended in divorce as in our day! That's a terrible indictment against the Christian community.

Decide right now that your marriage won't become a divorce statistic. You can make it work, because true love starts with a decision, not a feeling. If past hurts have caused you to think you don't love your spouse anymore, with God's help, you can make the decision to learn to love him or her all over again.

Some Christians try to rationalize getting a divorce by saying, "I just married the wrong person. I need to get a divorce so I can marry the right person and get back in God's perfect will." But that's a lie from the devil! If you're married, you're married to the right person. God honors the marriage covenant and wants you to make it work by walking in love with your mate according to the Word.

In order to make your marriage work, *never take your spouse for granted.* Without his or her support and help, you'll never make it in the ministry.

Too often people in the ministry give of themselves to others all day long and then come home tired and grumpy, ready to yell at their spouse and children, especially if anything goes wrong. But the truth is, a person should treat his spouse and children better than he treats anyone else!

If you're going to make your marriage work, *you must make a continual effort to keep the lines of communication open between you and your mate.* Don't just talk about practical matters, like the monthly budget. Make it a point to find time to talk to one another about the important issues of life. Learn to share from your heart about the things you think about and feel.

For instance, if a husband is called to the ministry and attends Bible school while his wife stays home with the children, he should be sure to take time to share with her what he's learning. She's a part of his ministry, too, whether or not she ever preaches from a pulpit. And both of them can grow closer in their relationship as they study and discuss the Word together.

get your family in agreement with **GOD**'s call

It's vital that your spouse be in agreement with you as you answer the call of God on your life. Until you're both in agreement to obey God's call, you'll struggle in the ministry.

I remember one woman who only *mentally* agreed with her husband's call to the pastoral ministry. Even though she said she was ready to be a pastor's wife, she wasn't *spiritually* hooked up with him at all.

Later this woman's husband accepted a pastorate of a church. One day his wife said, "This isn't what I thought the ministry would be like. I don't want to be in the ministry! I want you to have a regular job so you can be home with me and the children in the evenings."

Because this woman was pulling against her husband's call to the ministry, she not only created a problem in the church, she also hindered her husband's efforts to do what God had called him to do.

So do everything you can to come into agreement with your spouse. Once you and your spouse make a quality decision to obey the call of God together, it'll be much easier to withstand Satan's pressures against your family.

Getting in agreement with your spouse is also a part of wisely managing your home. Some people experience problems in their marriage and family because they've never managed their home properly. They do things in a slipshod way, with no thinking or planning, and they fail to set common goals.

Of course, the most important goal for a family to discuss is that of obeying God's call to the ministry. You see, entering the ministry is really a family matter, because it calls for changes that affect every member of the family.

So get your family involved in your call to the ministry. Make it a *team* effort. Talk with them about the price and the rewards of obedience to God.

When you make your spouse and children a vital part of your decision to answer your call, it will help the whole family become unified so you can all work together to obey God.

ministry is a lifestyle

As I've said, your family must be unified as you enter the ministry. Although ministry is a great privilege and perhaps the most *gratifying* profession anyone could be called to, it's also probably the most *difficult* profession in the world. Your family's support and willingness to obey God will make it much easier for you to successfully overcome the natural and spiritual pressures that will arise.

You see, ministry is a lifestyle, not just a nine-to-five job. Once you enter the ministry, to a large extent, your time isn't your own anymore.

When you're in the ministry, time becomes one of your most precious commodities. For the rest of your life, you're going to spend much of your time ministering—first to your family and then to others. That's why it's important to learn to budget your time, just as you budget your finances.

It's important to help your family understand the life-style and demands that go along with being in the ministry. Because you may be on call to minister to people when they need you, it's often difficult to set a predictable routine your family can always follow and depend upon.

Be sure your family understands that every day is different in the ministry. For example, as an associate pastor, I once spent most of the night at a hospital ministering to a seriously ill church member. I returned home the next morning just in time to change clothes and leave to attend a ministers' conference.

When that meeting was over, I came back to the church to take care of some church business. Then I returned to the hospital to check on the sick person. His condition had worsened, so I stayed at the hospital until 2 a.m.

That's just how some days go in the ministry, and there will be times when your family just has to "go with the flow"!

Make your family aware that being in the ministry is sometimes like living in a fishbowl! You're constantly under the scrutiny of other believers, as well as the public. And sometimes, it seems as though everyone in the world is watching you.

For instance, I can't even go to a store to buy a pair of socks without someone saying something like, "Hello, Rev. Hagin. So this is the brand of socks you like!" But that's just part of accepting the call to ministry.

Certainly, a minister and his family should enjoy times of quiet and privacy together. On the other hand, they can't isolate themselves in their own little world just because they don't want others watching them. The minister is called to set an example of godliness and make himself available to minister faithfully to others.

don't neglect your children

It's so important that you don't neglect your children as you answer your call to the ministry. Because there are so many demands and pressures on your time and energies, you must make a conscious effort to be certain you meet your children's needs. It's just too easy to minister to the needs of others at the expense of your own children.

If you want to have a close relationship with your children when they're older, you have to spend time with them when they're young. Give your children a lot of quality time and love. Love and attention are much more important than anything else you can give them.

If you ask the children of wealthy parents what they want most, they usually say they'd rather have their parents' love and attention than money and gifts.

I remember one boy who told me, "When I was young, my parents always gave me money and said, 'Go and have fun.' But what I really wanted was for them to sit down and color in a coloring book with me or play a game."

So no matter what your responsibilities are in ministry, be sure to be involved with your children's lives. Make it a point to enjoy activities with them that they're interested in.

For instance, take the time to play games with your children. If your children are involved in sports, arrange your schedule so you can watch their games or even coach their sports team.

I'm not telling you to do anything I haven't done. For instance, I coached my son's football team for many years. And my wife and I always made a point of being at our children's school and sports activities whenever we could, even if it meant sacrificing other important activities.

You, too, may have to sacrifice something else so you can be there when your family needs you. You may even have to lay aside some ministerial responsibilities so you can meet a need that arises in your children's lives. Remember, your spouse and children are your *number one* responsibility.

Strive to keep the channels of communication open with your children. Always make yourself available to them. Be accepting of their opinions and feelings so it's easy for them to confide in you.

Lynette and I always tried to maintain good communication with our children. And today we have great relationships with our children because the door of communication has always been open to them.

For instance, when my children were growing up, I let them know that if I was studying in my study, they could come in any time they wanted and talk to me. I'd always stop what I was doing and listen intently to what they had to say, because my children are very important to me.

I've known some ministers who tell their children, "I'm studying! Leave me alone." But if they aren't careful, they'll cause their children to rebel against them *and* God, because they aren't giving their children the time and attention they need.

I'll give you another example of how I kept the door of communication open between me and my children. When Craig was little, he and I had a bedtime routine. I'd sit on Craig's bed, and we'd discuss whatever was on his mind. Those little sessions before Craig went to sleep were set aside as a father-and-son time to talk.

As Craig grew to be a teenager, the bedtime talk was still an important part of our relationship. Sometimes Craig would come in from a date at night, peek his head in the door, and ask me, "Dad, are you still awake?" Even though I was often bone-tired, I'd always say, "Sure, come on in."

Craig would sit on the floor next to my bed and talk to me about what was going on in his life. He'd confide his feelings and thoughts about things that were important to him, and I'd always listen and try to help him any way I could.

But you don't achieve that kind of communication with your children overnight. You have to work at developing an intimate relationship with them, and you start when they're babies.

be considerate of your children's desires

It's also important to be considerate of your children's desires. Help them realize they're an important part of the family. Whenever possible, let *them* make choices. For instance, on occasion, let them choose where the family goes out to eat or what the family does on an outing.

Whenever possible, include the children in your discussion about where to go when planning a family vacation. Many times parents don't listen to what their children want to do. And because the family isn't in agreement about where to go for vacation in the first place, the family vacation becomes a time of fussing and arguing.

I'll never forget one family vacation when we went to Disneyland. I had to take my son's desires into consideration before my own. The children had excitedly anticipated this particular vacation for a long time.

When we first got to California, we stopped to visit one of my Bible school buddies. Without thinking, I asked him and his family to go along with us to Disneyland.

But my son, Craig, who was in junior high school at the time, was upset that I'd invited my friend to come along. Craig told me, "Dad, I thought this was supposed to be our family time together."

Enjoying our time in Disneyland alone as a family was really important to Craig. I realized I needed to consider his desire, so I told my friend, "Hey, I made a mistake. This is supposed to be our family outing. I'm sorry, but I shouldn't have invited anyone else to go with us."

My friend wasn't offended. He's a father too, and he understood the need for families to enjoy quality time together alone.

So I took the family to Disneyland, and we had a wonderful time that we'll remember for the rest of our lives. And Craig came home from that vacation realizing more than ever that his parents respected his desires and considered him an important part of the family.

When your children are teenagers, it's even more important to let them have a voice in the family and to consider their desires. Sometimes your teenagers have the right to be heard before you and your spouse make major decisions. If you always ignore their feelings and desires, you'll end up having to deal with rebellious teenagers, and it will be your own fault!

I learned that principle from my parents when I was a teenager. For example, when I was a junior in high school and my sister, Patsy, was a sophomore, our parents discussed with us the possibility of Mom traveling with Dad in the ministry for a year. That meant Patsy and I would have to go to a boarding school.

But Dad and Mom didn't just tell us, "You don't have any choice. You're going to boarding school whether you like it or not." They told us the decision was ours to make. If Patsy and I decided we wanted to go to public school that year, Mom said she'd stay home with us.

Patsy and I appreciated the opportunity to make that choice ourselves. That way we had no one to blame but ourselves if we didn't like the consequences of our decision. We made the decision to go to a private boarding school instead of to public school. As it turned out, it was a great school year.

Finally, be especially sensitive to your teenagers' feelings if they are seniors in high school. If answering the call to ministry means uprooting your teenager from his high school in his senior year, it would be good to prayerfully consider the possibility of waiting one more year before you move your family.

When you try to understand and consider *your children's* needs and desires, they'll be more understanding of *you* when you obey God in the ministry and it affects them personally.

I've shared some practical guidelines to help you guard your family in the midst of the demands of the ministry. Remember, your ministry will only be as successful as your marriage and your family life, so make your spouse and your children your highest priority. Treat them with loving care and thoughtfulness, working hard to make your home life the very best it can be.

And when the pressures and demands of ministry threaten to steal the peace of your home, don't let the devil catch you unawares and defeat you! Tap into God's power supply—His anointed Word—together as a family. Take authority over the enemy's strategies and claim God's promises in faith.

Trust the Lord with all your heart, and He *will* give you the wisdom and strength you need to guard your family in the midst of the pressures of ministry. He'll make a way for you to be everything you need to be to your family *and* fulfill your ministry too!

what is
success in the ministry?

ask any minister if he'd like to be successful in the ministry, and he'd say, "Of course!"

But what *is* success in the ministry? On the day you stand before Jesus, the Head of the Church, how will He determine whether you were successful in fulfilling your call?

let **GOD** take care of the results

To measure success the way God does, you must first forget about crowds and numbers. Great attendance in a meeting doesn't mean anything to God if He never told you to preach at that meeting in the first place. What really matters in determining your success with God is, *are you doing what He's told you to do?*

Too many ministers are caught up in the numbers game—how many attended church Sunday morning or how many were born again in their church. Pastors sometimes even try to impress other pastors by boasting about large church attendance. They brag, "We had 1,700 in church Sunday morning—and that didn't include 800 children!"

Thank God for the number of people who are born again and coming to church! But it isn't your responsibility to add up the results of your ministry! Your responsibility is to share the Gospel with people. It's God's responsibility to take care of the results and bring in a harvest of souls.

So quit looking at numbers! Get a vision of what God wants *you* to do in the ministry and then set out to obey Him. Don't try to make anything happen in your own strength. Just do what God tells you to do.

Someone may say, "Well, I'm doing what God told me to do, and I don't see any results." That's all right! If you're doing what God told you to do, then He's pleased with you. In His eyes, you're a success!

God doesn't require you to produce instant results or be an overnight success. Actually, it's *man* who is always looking for instant results—especially in this day and age!

But did you ever notice that a person who plants an orchard has to wait several years before he harvests any fruit off those trees? Suppose two years after a person planted his orchard, he checked to find fruit on his trees. He wouldn't find any, because the trees hadn't matured yet. But suppose he concluded, "Well, these trees aren't any good!" and cut them all down. Obviously, he'd never get any harvest!

No, if a person wants to be successful planting an orchard, he has to nurture his trees several seasons first. He has to feed them, spray them, and water them for several years until they reach a certain maturity. Then if he faithfully cares for them, the time will come when he will reap an abundant harvest for all his efforts.

In the same way, many times in your ministry you won't see the results you'd like to see right away. Often, some of the best fruit from your ministry will come years later.

For instance, a pastor may stay at a church and preach the Word for several years and not see a lot of results in people's lives. But he needs to trust the Lord with the results. As he's faithful to minister the Word to people week after week—diligently nurturing and watering his "crop"—one day he *will* see a harvest of good fruit in people's lives, and it will be the Lord's doing.

let **GOD** develop your ministry in his time

Make up your mind to do what God has told you to do and forget about the results and the numbers. Let God develop your ministry in *His* time, not yours.

Someone may protest, "Yes, but I want to build up my congregation to so many members in a certain length of time." But make sure that's *God's* goal, not just *your* goal.

If God gave you a certain timetable for church growth for your ministry, fine! Keep it to yourself, and let *Him* do it. Don't start manipulating circumstances, trying to make success happen by yourself.

The same thing is true when someone gives you a personal prophecy about your ministry. First, it must bear witness with your own spirit. But don't try to make a word from the Lord come to pass in your own strength. If the prophecy is really from the Lord, it will come to pass when God is ready for it to happen. But God will get you in position first before He brings it to pass.

Some believers dwell so much on personal prophecies that they try to make them come to pass in their own strength. And then after they've messed up what God wanted to do and things don't happen the way they were prophesied, those believers get disgruntled and frustrated. If it's from God, let *Him* do it. He's big enough to do what He promised.

Also, don't try to promote yourself in the ministry; trust God to promote you when you're ready. In the Book of Acts and in the Epistles, you don't find the apostles promoting themselves. They weren't egotistical. Not one of them was puffed up with pride over what *he* accomplished.

For instance, you won't find Paul boasting, "I preached to thousands when I was in Asia Minor. I've built churches all over the known world!"

Instead, you find Paul saying, "*Forgetting* what lies behind, I press *forward*" (Phil. 3:13). And you find him saying, "*. . . I determined not to know ANYTHING among you EXCEPT JESUS CHRIST and HIM CRUCIFIED*" (1 Cor. 2:2).

So don't get ahead of God and try to make something happen by promoting yourself. Just let God's purposes for your life happen in *His* timing. Do the best you can with the responsibility God has given you right now, but hold on to the vision God has given you for your ministry.

Dissatisfaction with your present situation will hinder you from entering into God's future plans for you. If you can't be satisfied with *today*, you're never going to experience what God has for you *tomorrow*! So make up your mind to be content and fruitful to God's glory in your present position as you obey God from a willing heart.

Do you know the best way to stay satisfied and fulfilled as you stand in faith for God to bring His purposes to pass in your life? Learn to delight yourself *in the Lord*. Unfortunately, some people mistake this for delighting in what they want God to give them.

Sometimes you can tell by the way people talk that they're only delighting in what God has given them, instead of delighting in the Lord Himself.

For instance, every time some believers share a testimony, it's always about the *material* things they've received from the Lord. They hardly ever say anything about the blessing of just personally knowing God or about people they're reaching with the gospel message.

There is a big difference between being thankful for what God has given you and only delighting in His material blessings. God doesn't want you to set your affections on the things of this world (1 John 2:15). He wants you to delight in *Him*.

As you seek God with all your heart, just wanting to know Him and obey His will, you open the way for Him to pour out His blessings on you. That's how you successfully fulfill the call of God on your life.

do what **GOD** has told *you* to do

Are you doing what you should be doing right now to fulfill God's call on your life?

To answer that question, ask yourself these questions: *Am I diligently doing what I know God has told me to do? As God has revealed to me each step to take, have I diligently obeyed Him to the best of my ability?*

If you can answer "yes" to those questions, then in God's eyes you are a success—even if you only have three people in your congregation, and two of them are asleep!

Don't try to measure your success by carnal measures, such as what kind of car you drive, the size of your congregation, or how many books and CDs you've produced. None of that means anything if you're not doing what God told *you* to do.

For instance, what good does it do to write a number-one bestseller, if you're miserable on the inside because God never told you to write it!

Also, success in the ministry isn't measured by whether a person has a pulpit ministry or a big congregation. Some people will never pastor a large congregation, because God has called them to pastor small churches.

Other people aren't called to preach or teach in a pulpit ministry. They're called to a helps ministry. Thank God for the ministry of helps! There's no way a preacher can accomplish the vision God has given him by himself; he needs the ministry of helps.

Christians need to realize that the helps ministry is a valid ministry. The ministry of helps has been underrated and not esteemed as it should be. Many helps ministers feel guilty that they aren't behind a pulpit, even though the helps ministry is exactly what God has called them to.

Everyone isn't called to a fivefold ministry. Some people are called to work in the ministry of helps, and they are vital to the Body of Christ. We can see this is true in the Scriptures. For instance, the ministry of helps is listed with several other important ministries in the Book of First Corinthians.

1 CORINTHIANS 12:28
28 And God has appointed these in the church: first apostles, second prophets, third teachers, after that miracles, then gifts of healings, HELPS, administrations, varieties of tongues.

The ministry of helps may include working full time helping a minister. But it can also include working at a secular job and helping a minister in your spare time. For instance, you might help a church with administrative work, carpentry, teaching, ushering, or working with children or youth.

Still others are called to be associate pastors. Some associate pastors would be out of God's will if they tried to be senior pastors.

Someone once asked one of my associate pastors, "When are you going to go into your own ministry?" My associate answered, "I *am* in my ministry."

The other person said, "Oh, you know what I mean. When are you going to become the head pastor of a church?"

My associate pastor said, "This is the ministry God told me to fulfill. Until God tells me to be the senior pastor of a church, I'll be an associate to the best of my ability!" Thank God for good associate pastors who are committed to support the pastor!

The Lord doesn't measure success in the ministry the way man measures success. When you stand before Jesus, He won't ask you, "How many people did you preach to?" or "How big was your church?" He'll only ask you, "Were you faithful to do what I called you to do?"

So if you want to be sure you can confidently say to Jesus, "Yes, I was faithful, Lord," then get on your face before God. Seek Him diligently to find out what His will is for *you.*

As you wait before the Lord in prayer, don't listen just for what you *want* to hear. For instance, you may be hoping to hear the Lord say, "Go pastor that big, prosperous church in such-and-such a town." But what if He tells you, "Go to that small town and start a church without any promise of salary"?

It's easy to talk yourself out of doing God's will and make excuses why His plan won't work. That's especially true when He's telling you to do something your flesh doesn't want to do!

But if you want to be successful in the ministry, you must put your flesh under and willingly obey God, no matter what He tells you to do. I guarantee that someday you'll be glad you did. God's plans are always best, and He always rewards obedience.

If you're serious about understanding God's will for *your* ministry, be sure you're not just copying what other ministers are doing. You'll never experience success in the ministry by starting programs just because others are.

Ministers often make that mistake. Especially in Charismatic circles, it's common for ministers to copy other ministers' programs and follow after the current spiritual fad. But ministers set themselves up for frustration and failure when they start programs just because it's the popular thing to do.

Sometimes to add credibility to their decision to start a certain program, pastors tell their congregation, "I believe *the Lord* wants us to do this." But if the Lord didn't tell them to do it, the program will fail.

Then when the program fails, their congregation says, "I thought you said the Lord told us to do this!" But because ministers are often afraid to admit, "I'm sorry; I missed it," they try to justify their decision and just dig themselves a deeper pit.

If a minister keeps making the same mistake of starting programs without the Lord's leading, the congregation eventually becomes disillusioned with his leadership. When people watch the programs he initiates fizzle out one after another, they eventually lose confidence in his ability to hear from God.

Many times when ministers get themselves trapped in this kind of a difficult situation, they get so frustrated, they want to quit the ministry. I've seen it happen! If only they'd listened to the Lord in the first place! But they made a mess of it when they decided to do something God never called them to do.

The Lord once told me, "If you're doing *anything* that takes your time and money away from what I've told you to do, you're in disobedience." That's a profound statement, and we all need to heed it!

So get it clear in your mind. Just because a program works for some ministers doesn't mean it's God's plan for *your* ministry. Programs are only good if that's what God has told *you* to do.

For example, it's not God's plan for every church in America to have early-morning prayer meetings. That may be fine for some churches because God told them to do it. But as I heard one minister say, "If an early-morning prayer meeting isn't the vision God has given the pastor and his congregation, after a few months, all they're going to end up with is a tired church!"

A program that works for one ministry may be an utter failure for another ministry. For instance, some pastors go to every church-growth seminar they can to find ways to increase the size of their congregation. But after implementing the suggested church-growth programs, they often end up *losing* people instead. That wasn't the Lord's plan!

Then these pastors get frustrated and discouraged because nothing seems to help their church grow. They don't seem to understand that the only thing that will help is to seek God for themselves and find out what He wants *them* to do.

Be careful to begin only new programs in your ministry that God has specifically told you to implement. Don't let others push you into doing something God did not tell you to do.

For instance, a pastor shouldn't establish a day-care center in his church just because people in his congregation tell him it's a good thing to do. If God wants a church to start a day-care center, He'll deal with the pastor—the one in authority. If the pastor is uncomfortable with the idea of a church day-care center, he shouldn't start one until he *knows* God wants him to do it.

The point I'm making is this: Seek God in the Word and in prayer long enough to know what His will is for your life and ministry. Don't take the easy way out and follow popular spiritual trends just because everyone else is doing it. Determine to find out God's will for you and your church, and then do it!

recognize your limits and limitations

An important aspect of achieving success in the ministry is *to recognize your limits and limitations*. When you understand your limits, you won't get frustrated by placing unrealistic expectations on yourself.

Of course, God has no limits or limitations. If it were only up to Him, the whole world could be reached for Jesus in a moment's time!

But God works through people like you and me, and we *do* have limitations. As ministers, we must learn how to work within the boundaries of those limitations so we can reach our highest potential.

First, you are limited in *time*. You only have so many hours in a day to accomplish what God has told you to do. If you start adding extra pursuits God didn't tell you to do, it will be at the expense of your first priorities—your relationship with God, your family, and your ministry.

For example, some pastors try to operate a business and pastor a church at the same time. I'll be honest with you. In that kind of situation, most of the time the pastor is going to end up feeling pulled in two different directions. As a result, both the business and the church usually suffer.

I'm not talking about a minister who has to work at a secular job when he's just starting out in the ministry, so he can provide for his family. There's nothing wrong with that. But once a person's ministry is established, if he's so consumed with outside pursuits that his family and his ministry suffer, then something is wrong!

Not only can you overextend yourself with pursuits *outside* the church, you can also get involved with too many activities *inside* the church. You may find yourself teaching and preaching in so many Bible studies and services during the week that you don't have time to prepare yourself properly for *any* of them.

There's certainly nothing wrong with serving people through the various outreaches in your church or ministry. But remember, you can only do so much. You can't win the world by yourself. God never asked you to. He just wants you to do what He's called *you* to do.

Second, you're limited by your *resources*. Your resources are the people, facilities, and equipment that are available to you for your ministry. You should always work within your available resources. At the same time, however, you should also believe God for *increased* resources.

For instance, a pastor shouldn't try to initiate a church-growth outreach if his church building is already too small! It's a known fact that most people won't come to church if it's more than 80 percent full, and they have to scramble for seats. So if the pastor tries to attract new church members before he's acquired extra space, when his church is 80 percent full, attendance will fall off.

Therefore, the pastor's first step should be to encourage the congregation to exercise their faith for a larger church building. After the church has moved into a larger building, the pastor can then start a program to increase the size of his congregation.

Third, you're limited in your *energy*. You can only keep up a fast pace for so long in ministry without resting. You only have so much energy. If you keep up a hectic schedule and never rest, it will eventually catch up with you. You'll become old and worn out before your time.

Some ministers experience spiritual and physical burnout because they're always on the go trying to keep up with all their responsibilities, outreaches, and programs.

They don't enjoy the ministry any more because they're exhausted, yet they never take time off to replenish their energy.

My dad learned early in his ministry that he only had so much energy and that he couldn't win the world by himself. So he did what God told *him* to do, and he let others do what God told *them* to do. Because Dad wisely stayed within the limits of his energy and resources, he kept going strong in ministry for nearly 70 years!

Fourth, you're limited in your *knowledge*. You don't know everything. For instance, you don't know everything about the Bible, and you don't know the answers to everyone's questions and problems. It's humanly impossible, so why try to pretend you know it all?

Sometimes the hardest thing for ministers to realize is that it's all right to say, "I don't know"! Some ministers like people to think they have an answer for everything. So when someone asks them a question and they don't know the answer, they talk in circles, trying to make the person think they know something—when they don't!

My dad often said that the more he learned about God's Word, the more he realized how much he didn't know!

Personally, I don't try to be an expert on everything. But when people ask me questions and I don't know the answer, I try to tell them where they can get the answer. For instance, I may tell them, "I know someone who has studied that subject. I'll talk to him and see if we can find an answer."

A minister doesn't have to be a know-it-all. Just be honest when you don't know the answer to someone's question. Meanwhile, trust God to increase your insight and wisdom in the things of God. Continue to *"Be diligent to present yourself approved to God, a worker who does not need to be ashamed, rightly dividing the word of truth"* (2 Tim. 2:15).

Fifth, you're limited in the *goals* you can set for your ministry. For instance, a pastor's goal for church growth generally is limited by the number of people living in the community. If there are only 300 people in the entire town, he probably can't expect a congregation of 3,000 people! In a situation like that, a congregation of 70 should be considered a great success, because that's a high percentage of the town's total population.

So learn to recognize your limits and limitations as you endeavor to fulfill the call of God on your life. When it seems as though you have failed, you may find you did nothing more than bump up against one of your limitations. If that's true, and you were honestly trying to obey God, you probably didn't fail at all.

apparent failure turned into success

Sometimes failure in the ministry is in the eyes of the beholder. For instance, suppose a congregation won't follow the pastor as he tries to fulfill the vision God has given him for the church. Suppose God's purpose for that church is never fulfilled, and God eventually tells the pastor to move on to another church. Some people would say that the pastor failed.

But God doesn't see that as a failure. A minister hasn't failed if he's done everything he can to obey God, but the congregation refused to obey God.

Sometimes what seems to be a failure in the ministry turns out to be a doorway to your greatest success. That happened in my own life. In 1972, I left an excellent position as an associate pastor to come to Tulsa and help my dad in the ministry.

At the time, that change of direction seemed like a step backward to me. If I had stayed at that church as an associate pastor, today I could be the senior pastor. Just before I left that position, I was preaching every Sunday and was totally involved in the operation of the church. I was also beginning to be recognized at the district level of the denomination.

Instead, the Lord led me to join my dad, Kenneth E. Hagin, as his crusade director. For several months, I didn't have one opportunity to preach. I was in charge of practical matters, such as loading and unloading trailers, working at book tables, and paying the crusade bills.

It looked as though I had gone backward in the ministry. Some people who didn't understand God's plan said, "Ken can't find anywhere else to minister, so he's going to work for his daddy. He isn't even preaching anymore!" But my move to Tulsa to help Dad turned out to be the greatest move I've ever made in my life. God has blessed my obedience beyond what I ever could have imagined.

When you're obeying God, it may sometimes look as if you're going backward. But if you know God has told you to step out in a certain direction, just obey Him. He knows what He's doing. Stay with Him and do only what He tells *you* to do. Then watch Him turn situations around for your good and make you a success in the ministry!

preach
the word!

n three words, I can give you one of the most practical guidelines you'll ever learn for success in the ministry: *Preach the Word!*

Don't preach your own opinion or someone else's opinion or experience. Don't preach the newest revelation or spiritual fad. Be sure everything you preach and do is in line with God's Word. That's the way to always stay on course as you endeavor to fulfill your call to the ministry.

I wish more ministers understood the importance of preaching only what stands the test of God's Word. Too many have gotten away from examining everything in light of the Word. As a result, many have fallen into doctrinal ditches.

doctrinal error is destruction from within the church

Whether you are a Christian who ministers from a pulpit or one whose ministry is outside the pulpit, you must stay alert to the devil's strategies to avoid getting into doctrinal error. Satan hasn't been able to conquer the Church from without, so he's trying to worm his way inside the Church and destroy it from within.

The devil is trying to cause people to lose confidence in Christian ministry by pushing unsuspecting ministers and lay-people into doctrinal extremes and error. Satan knows that if he can push believers into doctrinal error or extreme practices, they will be led *away from* God rather than *closer to* God.

doctrinal extremes in deliverance

If you'll just stay with the Word, you'll be able to recognize doctrinal errors when they surface. You see, the devil isn't imaginative. He causes the same doctrinal errors to appear again and again—they're just wrapped up in new packages. In fact, it's possible to trace some unscriptural doctrines in the Church today all the way back to the Early Church.

One doctrinal error that keeps reappearing is in the area of *deliverance*. I thoroughly believe that delivering people from demonic influence is scriptural. But some ministers get into error by teaching that a certain formula for deliverance has to be followed in every situation.

For instance, some teach that every person who's delivered from a demon must experience a physical manifestation, such as vomiting. Others teach that you have to pray for hours in tongues over a person for him to be delivered.

But nowhere in the Bible do I see that physical manifestations are a requirement for deliverance. Nowhere in the Bible are we told to pray in tongues to deliver someone from the devil. The only "formula" I find in the Word of God for casting out demons is "*Come out* in the Name of Jesus" (Mark 16:17; Acts 16:18)!

I traveled with my dad and watched him minister for years. Dad always stayed in line with the Word in the area of deliverance. In all those years of watching Dad minister, I never saw him deal with the devil in any way except by saying, "In the Name of Jesus Christ, I take authority over you!"

I never saw Dad pray or scream in tongues for hours to get someone delivered. Occasionally, physical manifestations occurred when someone was delivered. But I never heard Dad teach that a person who seeks deliverance *must* experience a physical manifestation to be delivered.

For instance, I've seen people fall under the power of the Holy Spirit after Dad told the devil to leave them in the Name of Jesus. But even though people fell under the power of the Spirit, Dad never taught that a person *had* to be delivered by falling to the ground!

The ministry of deliverance is necessary because so many people live as prisoners of the devil's bondage and oppression. You shouldn't back away from the ministry of deliverance just because some people take it to the extreme. But be careful to avoid doctrinal error by preaching what the *Word* says about deliverance.

doctrinal extremes in church government

Many people have also fallen into doctrinal extremes on the subject of *church government*. Christians have fought small wars over the question, "What is the scriptural form of church government?"

The Bible doesn't present a set formula for correct church government. But the Bible does make it clear that the pastor is the head of the local church (1 Peter 5:2).

Some people today advertise themselves as apostles or prophets and try to take the authority of the local church out of the pastor's hands. That's an old error concerning church government that has resurfaced in recent years.

But nowhere does the Bible say someone who calls himself an apostle or prophet can tell the pastor of a local church what to do!

I've seen advertisements that proclaim, "Prophet So-and-so is coming to town! Come and watch him anoint prophets to the ministry!" But that's also unscriptural.

No man can lay his hands on anyone and *anoint* him as an apostle or prophet. *Man* doesn't call or anoint people to the ministry; *God* does! And although man may help confirm what God has already placed in someone's heart, *God alone* sets a person into a particular ministry office.

Despite these extremes concerning the offices of apostle and prophet, we can't do away with these ministry gifts because they're scriptural. The Body of Christ needs those whom God has called as apostles and prophets to function in their proper place according to the Word.

The abuse of authority is another error that some ministers have fallen into in the area of church government. No pastor, or any other minister for that matter, has the right to control the lives of others.

When ministers try to control people's personal lives and hinder them from obeying the leading of the Holy Spirit, something is very wrong. For instance, some ministers make people feel as though they're backsliding for wanting to leave their church or doctrinal "camp." But the Bible says to ministers: *"Shepherd the flock of God which is among you . . . NOR AS BEING LORDS OVER THOSE ENTRUSTED TO YOU, but being examples to the flock"* (1 Peter 5:2–3).

Submission and authority in the local church is certainly a scriptural principle. But ministers should stay in line with the Word and lead the people by their godly *example*, not by force, or intimidation.

get back to the basics

I've mentioned just a few examples of doctrinal errors or extremes some Christians fall into. As Christians who minister, we have a responsibility to avoid these errors and stand on the basics of God's Word, no matter what anyone else is preaching or teaching.

The Bible says those who minister are to help the saints grow and mature spiritually so they won't be tossed around by every wind of doctrine (Eph. 4:12,14). But too many ministers are pushing their own doctrines and creating problems in the Body of Christ instead of perfecting the saints by preaching the Word.

However, we can't throw out valid doctrines that are vital to our spiritual walk just because some ministers preach extremes and excesses. For example, prosperity is scriptural (Gal. 3:13,29; 3 John 2), even though that biblical truth has been pushed to extremes and abused by some. But that doesn't mean we should not walk in prosperity!

The Bible tells us that God wants to bless His people in every area of life, including the material and financial realms (2 Cor. 9:6–11; Phil. 4:19). Unfortunately, some ministers have taken that biblical principle to the extreme, teaching people to believe only for selfish desires. The way some preachers talk, if a person doesn't drive an expensive car, wear expensive clothes, and live in a mansion, he's weak in faith!

God's concern is not what kind of car you drive. What *He* cares about is that you're driving your car to *His* destination—to help people in need and to preach the Gospel!

Some Christians get caught up in extreme prosperity teachings, and the desire to believe for material possessions becomes so important to them that they lose sight of their real mission in life—to reach souls for Jesus.

I'm so thankful God wants His children to prosper and have their needs abundantly supplied! But when people start seeking material possessions instead of God's Kingdom, that means the prosperity teaching has been pushed to the extreme. That grieves God.

However, that doesn't mean we're supposed to jump into the ditch on the other side of the road and stop preaching that God wants to prosper His people! If we throw out that scriptural truth just because some have gotten into excess, we do a great disservice to God's people and hinder them from walking in the fullness of their inheritance and ministry potential in Christ.

We are ministers of the Gospel, and our main mission in life is setting the captives free with the saving truth of Jesus Christ (2 Cor. 5:18; 1 Tim. 2:4). We must steer clear of unbiblical doctrines and extreme teachings that would pull us off track.

It's important to concentrate on *preaching the Word.* We must get back to the basics of the Word and fill the world with the message, "Jesus saves! Jesus heals! And Jesus is coming again!"

The Body of Christ is too divided over minor doctrinal issues. As ministers, we can help that sad situation by doing all we can to maintain unity by walking in love with other believers. We may never all agree on every minor detail of doctrine. But we can agree on the major doctrines, such as salvation through Jesus Christ, the Son of God.

We are one Body under one Head—Jesus Christ. As we all build our foundation on the basic doctrines of God's Word, to a greater and greater degree, we'll be able to unite and work toward the common purpose of building God's Kingdom. Then the power of God will be manifested in our midst as never before.

don't look for new revelations

Some Christians are doctrinally fickle—always searching for new revelations or doctrines they can preach. They seem to think they constantly need to preach something new so people will think they've reached some high spiritual level. Too often, those "revelations" are teachings that go beyond the Word.

Certainly the Holy Spirit continually gives us more light as we study the Word. But we can get into error if we're always looking for some new revelation.

Personally, I've found that the more I study the Word, the more I see I've only scratched the surface of God's truth. But I also realize that new illumination in God's Word won't do me any good if I'm not walking in what God has already shown me!

God never takes us beyond His Word to give us some "greater revelation" that can't be found in the Bible.

Ministers who are always preaching new "revelations" try to tell you, "This is a higher teaching than the old, established teachers of the Word ever taught." For instance, at one time, there was a teaching in the Church that some of the older ministers should get out of the way so younger ministers could take over.

Those who taught this used Moses and Joshua as examples. Joshua may have known ahead of time what God wanted him to do. But Joshua didn't try to make that happen prematurely by forcing Moses out of his position as Israel's spiritual leader.

We would be in serious trouble if we suddenly removed all the Moseses—the older, seasoned ministers—from the Church and left only the younger ministers or Joshuas.

The Body of Christ desperately needs the old pillars of the Church. They've gone through some things as spiritual pioneers we will never have to experience if we will listen to them and receive the wisdom they've gained over the years.

Not only can we benefit from the many years of proven experience of these seasoned ministers, we can even learn from some of the mistakes they overcame. As a result, we should be able to stay on course.

We need older ministers who have been faithful to teach and establish the rest of us in the Word. And the older ministers need the younger generation of ministers so the work of the ministry can continue and the Gospel can go forth throughout the earth!

Don't let the devil take you on a wild goose chase by searching for some "higher revelation" to base your ministry on. And you don't need to get sidetracked into focusing on or arguing with those who preach things that are beyond the Word. Just stay out of strife, walk in love, and continue to preach the Word!

preach the *truth*

Don't spend all your time preaching against wrong doctrine. Don't waste your energy preaching *against*

something. Just concentrate on preaching *for* something—
the truth of God's Word.

When you preach the truth, the truth of God's Word
reveals doctrinal error. And if people are sincere about
serving God, God's Word will straighten out their thinking
in any area where they are believing wrong.

Just take a stand on God's truth and refuse to back
off from preaching the Word. Then people will either repent
and change, or they'll leave your church because they don't
want to change or deal with the conviction of the Holy
Spirit.

Also, as you determine to preach the truth, be sure
you aren't preaching someone else's message verbatim *just*
because you listen to their sermons and respect their ministry. Don't allow yourself to listen to the voices of so many
different ministers that you get confused about what's truth
and what's error.

Ask God to help you zero in on two or three seasoned
ministers who are established in the Word. Listen to them
and learn from them as long as they stay in line with God's
Word. But don't try to copy everything they say and do in
your own ministry.

preach as the Lord leads *you*

Thank God for recorded teaching and Christian books
that teach the Word! But don't just grab sermons you read
or hear and immediately try to preach them. If you do that
you're only parroting someone else.

Instead, study the subject in the Word yourself. Then
pray until that message becomes a burning fire in your own

heart. Only then will you be able to preach it with conviction and with the anointing of the Holy Spirit.

You put yourself in a box when you try to preach just like the ministers you most admire. Just be sure you're preaching according to the Word and with the anointing of the Holy Spirit. Then preach the way the Lord leads *you*. There's no greater satisfaction than to minister the Word from your heart, knowing you did what God told *you* to do.

Also, don't preach on subjects you don't understand. Don't try to teach others about things you haven't experienced in your own life. For instance, if you're not a parent, it would be hard for you to try to teach others how to raise children.

On the other hand, that doesn't mean you shouldn't teach on biblical subjects like healing just because you've never experienced a major healing. You can always preach and teach the Word. But if you try to teach something you don't understand or something that isn't real in your own heart, people will quickly find out you don't know what you're talking about!

When I was young in the ministry, I learned to keep my opinion to myself on some subjects. I waited until I had gained more experience in the ministry and knew what I was talking about before I preached on a particular subject. That's just practical wisdom.

There's a great value in the lessons you learn by going through tests and trials and coming out on the other side with a deeper assurance of the character and nature of God. Those lessons bring an added depth to your sharing of truth as you tell others of God's love and faithfulness. When you've actually experienced in your own life what you proclaim to others, then you're not just parroting what you've heard someone else say.

preach what people need

For those who minister from the pulpit, you not only have a responsibility to preach or teach the Word, you also need to find out what *God* wants you to preach every time you step behind the pulpit.

You need to be careful you don't get in a rut preaching the same 10 messages over and over again. People need a varied diet of the Word.

In the natural realm, people get sick if they eat only one kind of food all the time. The same principle is true in the spiritual realm. People will become spiritually sick if all you feed them is spiritual dessert. In other words, they'll eventually get spiritually weak in important areas of their Christian walk if you only preach on subjects that are easy for them to listen to, such as faith, healing, and prosperity.

For instance, sometimes people need to hear strong sermons on commitment and obedience! If you mention the subject of commitment in some churches, people start backing away in a hurry. But all believers must learn to be committed to obeying God if they're going to maintain their spiritual health.

Only God knows what a group of people needs at any given time. A sermon that really ministers to one group of people might not be what another group needs at all. So before you ever step up to the pulpit, get on your face before God and find out what *He* wants you to preach.

It's easy to preach what people think they *want* to hear. But be faithful to preach what people *need* to hear. And if you're a pastor, invite good ministers to preach in your pulpit from time to time who will also teach what your congregation needs to hear.

It's so important to stay on course with the Holy Spirit in your preaching. As you seek God, He will give you a fresh message every time you preach. And if you stay sensitive to the Holy Ghost, He'll move in your service to meet people's specific needs.

Make a lifetime decision to preach the *whole* truth of God's Word—not just the part that's easy for people to hear. Avoid doctrinal error or extremes at all costs. And always be sure you preach God's anointed message for the moment. When you make that kind of commitment, you establish a sure foundation for success in the ministry!

chapter eleven

anointed
with fresh oil

a s a minister of the Gospel, you are *anointed* to do what God has called you to do. God Himself equips and empowers you by His Spirit to do the work of the ministry. But that anointing isn't a one-time experience. If you want to fulfill your call successfully, *continual* fresh anointings or infillings of the Holy Spirit are a necessity, not a luxury.

David, who was called of God to *his* generation, understood that. David said, ". . . I shall be anointed with fresh oil" (Ps. 92:10 *KJV*). In the Bible, oil is a type of the Holy Spirit so David was actually saying, "I shall be continually anointed with the Holy Spirit."

natural oil versus the oil of the Holy Spirit

How does natural oil illustrate the anointing of the Holy Spirit? One way is that oil gets old and rancid after a while and needs to be replaced with fresh oil. For instance, restaurants can use the same pot of oil to fry foods for only a limited time; then, the oil must be changed. Otherwise, the food will taste stale or rancid.

Also, some oil is absorbed by the food and some evaporates as the food is cooking. So new oil must be frequently added to keep the right amount in the pot.

There are times when the pressures and problems of the ministry can make you feel as though you are in a boiling pot of oil with the heat turned up to "high"! In the midst of those pressures, you can't keep on ministering to people on the strength of old, stale oil—your past times of refreshing and close communion with God.

If you try to live on old, stale oil, your spiritual walk and your ministry will eventually lose its freshness and seem dead and stagnant. It's important to spend time with God *daily* in His Word and in prayer so you continually receive a fresh anointing of the oil of the Holy Spirit.

Sometimes when you feel drained of strength and energy, you may need to add a little more of the Holy Ghost's power to your supply. How? It's simple. Just go back to the One Who is the *Source* of that divine oil.

Meditate on the scriptures that promise you fresh infillings of the Holy Spirit (Ps. 92:10; Acts 2:4; 4:31; Eph. 5:18–19). Then minister to the Lord and thank Him for anointing you afresh with His Spirit. God will answer your prayer of faith by quickening your mortal body and strengthening you with might in the inner man by His Spirit (Rom. 8:11; Eph. 3:16).

I think it's easier to appreciate the work of the Holy Spirit when we understand that oil is a type and analogy of Him and then we look at various features of oil. For example, consider these two features or purposes of motor oil that help an engine run smoothly and keep the automobile ready to serve us.

First, the motor oil lubricates the engine parts to eliminate friction. Friction creates heat. Too much heat causes the motor to seize and lock up. When Satan turns up the heat in your life through problems and pressures, the fresh oil of the Holy Spirit eases the friction so pressures don't grind on your mind and emotions.

Second, as oil flows through the engine, it works as a cleansing agent to clean out impurities. The fresh oil of the Holy Ghost helps you respond to problems according to the Word instead of according to your flesh. And as you yield to the Holy Spirit's promptings within you, that divine oil also cleans out those areas in your life that are displeasing to God (Matt. 3:11–12).

the anointing oil of the old testament

In the Old Testament, God instituted the use of anointing oil to set a person apart to do a specific work or ministry for Him. Oil was a type of the Holy Spirit to consecrate and empower a person for service to God.

This anointing oil was not an ordinary oil. It was formulated by God for a holy, sacred purpose.

EXODUS 30:30–31
30 "And you shall ANOINT Aaron and his sons, and CONSE-CRATE them, THAT THEY MAY MINISTER TO ME AS PRIESTS.
31 "And you shall speak to the children of Israel, saying: 'THIS SHALL BE A HOLY ANOINTING OIL TO ME throughout your generations.'"

God told the Israelites exactly how to make the holy anointing oil (Exod. 30:23–25). Then He warned the Israelites that if anyone made or used the holy anointing oil for any other purpose than the one God intended, that person would be cut off from His people (Exod. 30:31–33).

When someone was anointed to do a certain work for God, the anointing oil was poured upon him from the hollowed-out horn of an animal (1 Sam. 16:13). All the oil in the horn was poured out on top of the person's head, and the oil flowed down over his head and face and onto his clothes (Lev. 8:12; Ps. 133:2). That symbolized the anointing of the Holy Spirit upon him to serve God.

What does the holy anointing oil in the Old Testament have to do with believers under the New Covenant? Under the Old Covenant, those who were called as prophets, priests, and kings were anointed and empowered *from without* to perform their task.

When we become believers through the New Birth under the New Covenant, the Holy Spirit dwells within our recreated human spirits (John 14:17). When Jesus baptizes us with the Holy Spirit, He fills us to overflowing with that Spirit (Matt. 3:11; Acts 2:4).

I like to describe that overflow this way: the precious oil of the Holy Spirit begins bubbling up *from within* until it flows out and anoints our outer man. Spiritually speaking, we can actually become *saturated* with the oil of the Holy Spirit.

anointed for ministry

There's also the anointing of the Holy Spirit upon those who are called to the ministry. Jesus talked about the anointing upon Him for service when He first started his ministry on this earth.

LUKE 4:18

18 "The Spirit of the Lord is upon Me, Because HE HAS ANOINTED ME TO PREACH THE GOSPEL to the poor; He has sent Me TO HEAL the brokenhearted, TO PROCLAIM LIBERTY to the captives And RECOVERY OF SIGHT to the blind, TO SET AT LIBERTY those who are oppressed.

Jesus was anointed—set apart, equipped, and empowered—by the Holy Spirit in His earthly ministry. In the same way, those who are called to the ministry today are anointed by the Holy Spirit to help build the Kingdom of God.

That anointing for ministry is not just upon you, as it was for the Old Testament prophets, priests, and kings. If the anointing were simply abiding upon you, it would wear off in a way similar to natural oil as it is used in your daily routine!

But because you're born again, the anointing of the Holy Spirit also abides *within* you. Since the Holy Spirit lives in you, He's *always* available to equip and empower you for service.

For instance, suppose you're a pastor and you're out playing baseball. Suddenly, you receive an emergency call that a church member has been taken to the hospital.

To minister effectively to the person, you must stir up the anointing within. You have to learn how to allow God to saturate your being with the fresh oil of the Holy Spirit at a moment's notice. Then you can go straight from the baseball field to the emergency room and minister in the power of the Holy Spirit. Similarly, whatever your calling is in ministry, you can stir yourself up by praying in the Spirit (1 Cor. 14:5; Eph. 5:18–19).

anointed for **GOD**'s service

Have you ever considered this—you are anointed to help carry on the earthly ministry of Jesus Christ (John 14:12; Acts 1:1). You are *not* anointed to build your own ministry.

When you come through difficult trials and hardships victoriously and begin seeing success in your ministry, do not adopt the attitude, *Look at what I did! Look at MY ministry!* No! No matter how successful you become, always remember that God is the One Who called, equipped, and anointed you! You can't take any credit for what He's done through you!

God is the One Who gave you the talents and abilities to succeed. All you did was yield yourself to Him and, at some point, say as Isaiah did, "Lord, here am I; send me!" (Isa. 6:8).

Then God took you, with all your human frailties and weaknesses, and fashioned you to be a blessing in and to the Body of Christ. He called and anointed you for service so that through you, people could be delivered from the chains of sin, sickness, and disease.

Sometimes other people make the mistake of judging whether a minister is successful by outward appearances. For example, they judge him by how homiletically correct his sermon is. Or they try to judge him by how good an orator he is. But the Bible says it's not by a man's might or power that God's work is accomplished. It's by *His Spirit* (Zech. 4:6).

That verse applies to the ministry too. Ministers can only affect people's lives for the Lord by the power and anointing of the Holy Spirit. They're not going to bring people to repentance just through their great oratorical skills. Ministers won't change people's lives by spouting off knowledge they learned at a university. They won't fulfill their ministry by any means other than the Spirit of God.

Yes, you can learn to be a good public speaker. But dynamic speaking alone isn't enough to reach the hearts of people. Only the Holy Spirit can touch people's hearts and change their lives.

For instance, a singer can have perfect pitch and a beautiful voice. But if he relies only on his natural talent instead of on the anointing of the Holy Spirit, people will leave the service in the same condition they came. They may comment on his beautiful singing, but their hearts will be untouched and unchanged by the power of God.

On the other hand, a simple, backwoods country boy who picks a guitar and sings with a whine in his voice can sing to the glory of God if the anointing of the Holy Spirit is upon him. His voice may be rough and unpolished, but if his singing is anointed by God, people's lives can be changed forever.

You see, ministers aren't *perfect*, but they're *anointed!* It's the anointing of the Holy Spirit upon ministers that makes the difference. Without the anointing, we can't accomplish a thing in the world for God.

never doubt the anointing upon you

Before you can be anointed with the *fresh* oil of the Holy Spirit, you need to know you've already been anointed by Him for the work of the ministry. The Bible says, *"Now HE WHO establishes us with you in Christ and HAS ANOINTED*

US IS GOD" (2 Cor. 1:21). You've been anointed by God for the ministry. You must take hold of that fact and *believe* you are anointed.

When you're in active ministry, it's important to believe you're anointed, so you can *act* on that knowledge by faith. For instance, when you know you're anointed to preach, then preach! Never doubt your anointing, no matter how you may feel or what obstacles may arise to oppose you.

Know that when God calls you to minister, He provides the equipment—the anointing to minister. Keep on ministering. Keep on serving His Kingdom. Keep on acting on that anointing. Just keep on preaching!

And furthermore, declare in faith as David did, "I have been and shall be anointed with fresh oil!" (Ps. 92:10). David didn't say, "I sure hope I've been anointed with oil. Maybe I'll be anointed with oil if it's God's will. Maybe I was anointed." No, he believed he *had been anointed* and declared boldly, "I *shall be anointed* with the fresh oil of the Holy Spirit!"

GOD's reservoir of oil never runs dry

David had no fear that God might someday run out of the oil of the Holy Spirit. David knew that with God, there's no shortage of divine oil.

You see, unlike man who struggles with finite resources, God has infinite resources. God doesn't have to explore for oil because He's running dry. He has a bottomless reservoir of Holy Ghost oil that *never* runs dry!

Not only that, but the price of God's divine oil never changes. It doesn't go up or down with man's economic whims. The price is always the same—it's a free gift from the Heavenly Father.

To obtain God's holy oil, all you have to do is go before the Throne of God and ask in faith, "Father, please anoint me with the fresh oil of Your Holy Spirit." You can rest assured that the fresh oil of the Holy Spirit will be available to strengthen and renew your spirit every time you need it.

fresh oil for today

Some ministers try to operate on yesterday's oil. When they do that, they experience unnecessary problems in their lives and ministry. The Israelites did the same thing. They created problems for themselves when they tried to live on yesterday's stale manna.

Exodus 16:15–20

15 So when the children of Israel saw it [manna—God's bread from Heaven], they said to one another, "What is it?" For they did not know what it was. And Moses said to them, "This is the bread which the Lord has given you to eat.
16 "This is the thing which the Lord has commanded: 'Let every man GATHER IT ACCORDING TO EACH ONE'S NEED, one omer for each person, according to the number of persons; let every man take for those who are in his tent.'"
17 Then the children of Israel did so and gathered, some more, some less.
18 So when they measured it by omers, he who gathered much had nothing left over, and he who gathered little had no lack. Every man had gathered according to each one's need.
19 And Moses said, "LET NO ONE LEAVE ANY OF IT TILL MORNING."
20 Notwithstanding THEY DID NOT HEED MOSES. But SOME OF THEM LEFT PART OF IT UNTIL MORNING, and IT BRED WORMS and STANK. And Moses was angry with them.

Some of the Israelites were afraid the manna would run out, so when they gathered their daily portion, they tried to store extra for the next day. But all they got for their trouble was a bunch of worms!

The Israelites had to learn to trust God to provide fresh manna from Heaven every day. For 40 years, God never failed them! He provided fresh manna for them every morning (Exod. 16:35).

We need to learn the same lesson! We can trust God to give us a fresh supply of the oil of the Holy Spirit faithfully every day.

God has a never-ending supply of divine oil. We don't have to try to store it up! All we need to do is receive a fresh supply each day. Each day's supply is enough to live victoriously for that day. Then we need to go back into the Presence of God to receive fresh oil for the next day.

When you try to live on yesterday's oil, you become spiritually dull and stale. You lose the fresh sense of God's Presence in your life which is important for ministry.

You see, yesterday's oil for ministry already did what it was supposed to do for *that* day. It eased the friction of yesterday's pressures and cleansed yesterday's impurities from your mind and emotions.

But you must be anointed with *fresh* oil *today*! A fresh anointing of the Holy Spirit daily helps keep you from experiencing friction and strife with your fellow man. The soothing power of that oil binds up and heals wounds inflicted on your heart or soul. And that fresh oil cleanses you from all impurities, so you can accomplish what God has called you to do *today*.

The fresh oil of the Holy Spirit also revives your spirit when you hit a low period in your life or when you feel spiritually dull or dry. You can go through a spiritual dry spell when you get out of tune with God. A fresh anointing of God's Spirit will help you tune in again to the Lord.

What do I mean by getting out of tune with God? You tune in to a certain radio station by turning the dial. The station comes in loud and clear when you're tuned in to the right frequency. If your tuning is off, you only pick up static.

Sometimes ministers aren't in tune with God the way they should be. For example, they may have grumbled and complained. Then when they encounter a problem, they cry, "Oh, God, I thought you called me to the ministry! But look at all the things that are going wrong! Why aren't You doing something about this mess?"

They need to repent and get back in tune with God so they can hear Him again! If they'll spend time in His Presence, they can receive a fresh anointing of the Holy Ghost. That will make it easier for them to trust in His faithfulness and stand fast on His Word, no matter what the circumstances look like. Once they're in tune with God again, they'll be too busy praising Him for His goodness to complain about anything!

We who are parents understand the importance of teaching our children not to complain. We don't allow our children to talk back to us.

For instance, when our family sat down to dinner, we didn't allow our children to grumble and complain about the food. We told them, "Eat what's set before you! This food is healthy, and it will make you strong." Yet how often do we complain and talk back to our Heavenly Father, saying, "God, why did You let this happen to me?"

Our Heavenly Father has prepared a spiritual banquet table before us that's full of blessings. But it's also full of responsibilities. It's important that we sit down at His table and eat what He has set before us—responsibilities and all—and stop griping about it!

In other words, we need to get on our face before God, receive His fresh oil, and then go forth with joy to do what He's called us to do. Simply obeying Him will make us spiritually strong and healthy so we can accomplish His purposes for the Kingdom of God.

fresh oil brings fresh vision

Your commitment to God to answer His call and obey Him must be renewed daily. Otherwise, the devil will try to find ways to make you neglect your commitment and doubt your call. The fresh oil of the Holy Spirit will give you a renewed confirmation of your call and help you stay true to your commitment to the Lord.

If you start doubting your call to the ministry, get before God and get an oil change! With a fresh anointing of the Holy Spirit, your divine call will be confirmed in you again. You'll come out of your time of prayer declaring, "I *am* called of God and anointed for the ministry of Jesus Christ!"

Fresh oil will help you complete the vision God has already given you. It will also give you fresh vision for the *future*. It takes fresh oil every day to accomplish the new tasks God gives you! Fresh opportunities to minister to people await you every day. Those opportunities can't be accomplished with old, stale oil.

So if you want to walk closely with the Lord day by day, determine to receive fresh oil every morning. Go to God daily in the Word and in prayer. Let the oil of the Holy Spirit revive your spirit and heal any hurts and wounds in your heart and soul. Pray until you can arise and say, "The Lord has anointed me with fresh oil!"

As you live each day anointed with fresh oil, the power and Presence of the Holy Spirit in your life and ministry will be as real and fresh today as when you first received the Holy Spirit.

the fire of revival is spreading!

I firmly believe we are now in the last days before Jesus returns to the earth. As we study the Word and look at the signs of the times, it's obvious that the end of the age is coming quickly.

Revival is spreading all over the world. It's going to be a greater revival than has ever before been seen on this earth. It will be easier and easier to get people saved, healed, and filled with the Holy Spirit. And as people hunger for the things of God, the Lord will confirm His Word to a greater degree through mighty signs and wonders!

It's time for us to realize that every single day, we, the army of God, must arise anointed with the fresh oil of the Holy Spirit. Without that daily fresh anointing, you'll be unprepared to accomplish the task God has called you to do in these last days. And without fresh oil, you won't be ready when Jesus returns.

Don't allow yourself to become complacent. Don't allow the fire of revival to die in your heart. If you fail to receive fresh anointings of the Holy Spirit and you let the fire go out, your ministry will perish in the smoke!

Personally, I'm tired of the smoke—people only talking about revival and demonstrations of the Spirit, but never experiencing God's power in their own lives. I don't want to just *talk* about the power of God! I want to live and operate my ministry in God's power every day of my life.

It's time to stop just *talking* about the miraculous power of God. It's time to get on our faces before God and receive a fresh anointing of the Holy Spirit! It's time to go forth in the power of a fresh anointing so you can stand against the onslaughts of the enemy. Let's show this hurting world that Jesus Christ is still alive!

renew your ministry

Renew your ministry and commit yourself afresh to God's call on your life. Decide that there aren't enough demons in hell or obstacles from Satan to keep you from fulfilling your ministry!

Never forget that your call to the ministry is a great privilege. There's truly no greater joy than to see sad, sick, lost people set free as you minister to them.

Personally, I believe there is no higher calling than the ministry of the Lord Jesus Christ. There is no better race to run than the race that's set before ministers of the Gospel. The Bible says, *". . . HOW BEAUTIFUL ARE THE FEET OF THOSE WHO PREACH THE GOSPEL OF PEACE, Who bring glad tidings of good things!"* (Rom. 10:15).

So determine that you're going to be faithful to your call until you finish your spiritual race. You're not just running a 100-meter dash. You're committed to the marathon—the ministry for life!

In a marathon, runners come to a point in the race where their lungs start hurting, their legs are aching, and everything in them is screaming that they can't take another step. Sometimes you feel like that in the spiritual race God has set before you too!

That's the time to determine, "I *will* finish my spiritual race! There is a crown of righteousness laid up for me (2 Tim. 4:8). And I *will* attain it, because I'm determined to fulfill God's call on my life!"

With that kind of determination to obey God and fulfill your call, the day will come when you'll look back on your life with great satisfaction. You'll be so thankful to God for helping you each step of the way. And you'll be able to say from your heart, "Faithful is my God Who called me! Praise His mighty Name! He has brought His purpose to pass in my life!"

about the **author**

Rev. Kenneth Hagin Jr., president of Kenneth Hagin Ministries and pastor of RHEMA Bible Church, seizes every ministry opportunity to impart the attitude of "I cannot be defeated, and I will not quit." He has ministered for almost 50 years, beginning as an associate pastor and traveling evangelist. He has organized and developed 14 RHEMA Bible Training Centers around the world and is the founding pastor of RHEMA Bible Church. With his wife, Rev. Lynette Hagin, Rev. Hagin Jr. co-hosts *Rhema for Today,* a weekday radio program broadcast throughout the United States, and *RHEMA Praise,* a weekly television broadcast.

To fulfill the urgent call of God to prepare the Church for a deeper experience of His Presence, Rev. Hagin Jr. emphasizes key spiritual truths about faith, healing, and other vital subjects. He often ministers with a strong healing anointing, and his ministry helps lead believers into a greater experience of the glory of God.